D1334630

Learnin

Edited by Fran

First published in Great Britain in 1998 by

The Policy Press
University of Bristol
34 Tyndall's Park Road
Bristol BS8 IPY
UK

Tel   +44 (0)117 954 6800
Fax   +44 (0)117 973 7308
E-mail tpp-info@bristol.ac.uk
www.policypress.org.uk

Reprinted 2002

In association with the ESRC *Learning Society Programme*

ISBN 1 86134 123 7

Frank Coffield is Professor of Education in the Department of Education at the University of Newcastle. He is also currently the Director of the ESRC's research programme *The Learning Society* (1994-2000).

Cover design by Qube Design Associates, Bristol.
Printed in Great Britain by Hobbs the Printers Ltd, Southampton.

Contents

Notes on contributors

Ms Jane Alderton is Senior Lecturer at the Institute of Nursing and Midwifery, University of Brighton. She has published research on knowledge use by nurses and midwives and interprofessional healthcare teams.

Professor David Ashton is the Director of the Centre for Labour Market Studies at the University of Leicester. The Centre specialises in Research, Consultancy and Postgraduate teaching in Human Resource Development (HRD). The Centre runs one of the largest distance learning courses in Training and HRD currently available, enrolling practising professionals in five continents and over 25 countries.

Mr Stephen Baron, a Senior Lecturer in the Department of Education, Glasgow University, has researched in the area of learning difficulties since 1980 and has published (with J.D. Haldane) *Community, normality and difference: Meeting special needs* (Aberdeen University Press, 1992). He is currently completing the manuscript *Community and control: Surveillance, containment and the state* (Addison, Wesley and Longman).

Dr Antje Cockrill is a Research Associate in the Centre for Advanced Studies in the Social Sciences and a Tutor in the School of Education, University of Wales, Cardiff. She recently completed a doctoral thesis at the University of Wales, Aberystwyth.

Professor Frank Coffield has been Professor of Education in the Department of Education at the University of Newcastle since April 1996, having previously worked at Durham and Keele Universities. He is currently Director of the ESRC's research programme into *The Learning Society* from 1994-2000. In 1997 he edited a report *A national strategy for lifelong learning* (Newcastle, Department of Education, Newcastle University).

Mr Gerald Cole is a Research Fellow at the University of Sussex. He is the author of bestselling books on management, and has researched into the teaching of business studies and the assessment of professional competence.

Ms Dominique Danau works at the European Centre for Work and Society.

Ms Isabelle Darmon is a member of the research team at the Tavistock Institute, London, studying 'Innovations in continuing vocational training: A comparative perspective' as one of the 14 projects which make up the ESRC's *Learning Society Programme*.

Professor Michael Eraut is Professor of Education at the University of Sussex Institute of Education and directed one of the projects entitled 'Development of knowledge and skills in employment', as part of the ESRC's *Learning Society Programme*. He has published widely in the areas of professional and vocational education and of different kinds of knowledge.

Ms Kari Hadjivassiliou is a member of the research team at the Tavistock Institute, London, studying 'Innovations in continuing vocational training: A comparative perspective' as one of the 14 projects which make up the ESRC's *Learning Society Programme*.

Professor Sheila Riddell, having previously worked as Dean of Arts and Social Science at Napier University, Edinburgh, took up the post as Professor of Social Policy (Disability Studies) at Glasgow University in 1997. Her publications include *Gender and the politics of curriculum change* (Routledge, 1992) and *Policy, practice and provision for children with specific learning difficulties* (Avebury, 1995).

Dr Peter Scott is currently Lecturer in Sociology at the University of Bath. He was, until recently, a research associate in the Centre for Advanced Studies in the Social Sciences and School of Education, University of Wales, Cardiff, where the research reported here was carried out.

Mr Peter Senker has been a Senior Researcher in the Science Policy Research Unit and, more recently, the Institute of Education at the University of Sussex. He has published widely in the training of engineers and is now a visiting professor at the University of East London.

Mr Reiner Siebert is currently the Project Manager and Transnational Relations Coordinator for Jobrotation at the Berufsförderungszentrum in Essen, a vocational training college in North Rhine-Westphalia, Germany. Previously, he was a Research Assistant in Vocational Training and Unemployment Studies at Duisburg University, a teacher and then Head of Department in Adult Education for Languages and Business Studies, and a teacher and counsellor for Career and Guidance Services.

Ms Elisabeth Sommerlad works as a researcher for the Tavistock Institute, London.

Dr Kirsten Stalker is a Senior Research Fellow at the Social Work Research Centre, University of Stirling, and has published widely on social work provision to disabled children and adults.

Mr Elliot Stern is the principal investigator of the research team at the Tavistock Institute, London, studying 'Innovations in continuing vocational training: A comparative perspective' as one of the 14 projects which make up the ESRC's *Learning Society Programme*.

Dr Jill Turbin was a member of the research team at the Tavistock Institute, London, studying 'Innovations in continuing vocational training: A comparative perspective' as one of the 14 projects which make up the ESRC's *Learning Society Programme*.

Ms Heather Wilkinson is currently Research Fellow on the ESRC project 'The meaning of the Learning Society for adults with learning difficulties'. Prior to this project Heather worked as a researcher in the Departments of Applied Social Science and Educational Research, Lancaster University.

Introduction: new forms of learning in the workplace

Frank Coffield

Why is learning suddenly so important? This is the stark but central question posed by Stephen Baron and his colleagues in Chapter 5, which is dedicated not only to answering that question but also to exploring the difficulties and barriers which individuals, groups and organisations run into (or create for themselves), even when they are keen to learn. David Ashton found, for instance, that in certain firms learning was thought to be "... unproblematic, a natural process which occurs of its own accord and therefore did not require any special support or consideration". In other organisations, managers did not need to be convinced of the need for continuous learning, but at the same time they did not know how to support (far less enhance) the learning of their employees by, for example, providing constructive feedback.

The practical importance of this collection of articles is summarised in Chapter 4 by Michael Eraut and his colleagues, who argue that individuals can be helped to become more capable learners and that managers "can be helped to take more responsibility for the quality and quantity of learning in the units which they manage ... by creating/sustaining a microculture which supports learning from peers, subordinates and outsiders ...". Michael Eraut's project is a detailed study of learning at work in three sectors: engineering, business and healthcare, and he set out to provide "empirical evidence about what, how, where and why people learn at work." The provision of such evidence will help to transform fashionable phrases such as 'the learning organisation' or 'lifelong learning' into practical ideas and methods which could enhance the quality of learning in British firms.

These are the kind of issues explored in this report on interim findings on skill formation emanating from a number of projects within the Economic and Social Research Council's (ESRC) *Learning Society Programme*. It is the first in a series of such reports which are to be published by The Policy Press over the next two years on such themes as comparative studies, research and policy and informal learning. The strength of each report lies in the attempt to bring together empirical and theoretical insights around themes central to the notion of a learning society. The Programme has already produced a contribution to the debate on lifelong learning, entitled *A national strategy for lifelong learning* (Coffield, 1997) and a collection of articles which explored the concept of a learning society in a special edition of the *Journal of Education Policy* (vol 12, no 5, November-December 1997). But the present report sees the first publication of empirical findings which from now on will begin to flow increasingly from the 14 projects which make up the Programme. This collection and its successors aim to make additional, important contributions to the public debate on lifelong learning which has been galvanised by the publication of the new Labour government's Green Paper, *The learning age*, in February 1998.

It may be appropriate to begin by briefly introducing the *Learning Society Programme* itself. The full title of the Programme is 'The Learning Society: Knowledge and skills for employment' and the original specification described it as follows:

The Programme is a response to the growing national consensus that the UK needs to transform radically its thinking and practice in relation to education and training if it is to survive as a major economic power with a high quality of life, political freedom and social justice for all its citizens.

The aim of the Programme is to examine the nature of what has been called a learning society and to explore the ways in which it can contribute to the development of knowledge and skills for employment and other areas of adult life. The Programme focuses on post-compulsory education, training and continuing education in a wide variety of contexts, both formal and informal.

The Programme consists of 14 projects, involving over 50 researchers in teams spread throughout the UK, from Belfast to Brighton. Each project has a different starting and finishing time and the Programme itself will run until March 2000. Five of the 14 projects present papers in this collection and the sixth contribution in Chapter 2 (on a different model of lifelong learning, first developed in Denmark and now being introduced into Germany and the UK) is evidence of the determination to learn from advances being made in skill formation by our partners in the European Union (EU).

The standard format for such an introduction, for which no doubt there already exists some computer software, is to write a paragraph or two on each chapter in the order it appears in the report. That procedure will *not* be followed here. Instead, three themes which run through the chapters will be developed to give the reader a flavour of the wide range of topics covered by the authors: international comparisons; differing conceptions of learning and of the learning society; and conflicts between trust and hierarchy within firms. This introduction will then conclude by drawing out from these six chapters some of the more obvious implications for policy. It should, however, be pointed out that the policy recommendations are not the central focus of this first report and that the third report in this series (*The implications of research on The Learning Society for policy* [working title], 1999) will deal explicitly with the links between research and policy. Similarly, the main methodology employed in the following chapters is qualitative with an emphasis on case studies. Subsequent reports will draw on more quantitative approaches, for example, the new national survey of skills and economic rewards in a representative sample of the British workforce which was commissioned by the *Learning*

Society Programme and is being conducted by Francis Green, David Ashton and Alan Felstead.

Most of the projects within the Programme have incorporated a strong comparative dimension into their research design and that is particularly true of three of the studies in this report. So the first common theme is: how does the UK emerge from these comparisons between, for example, the construction industry in Wales and Germany (Chapter 1), the Jobrotation initiative in Germany and throughout the EU, including the UK (Chapter 2), and innovations in company training in England, France and Spain (Chapter 3)?

Peter Scott and Antje Cockrill conclude in the first chapter that much of the British construction industry "clings grimly to an informal mode of poorly accredited 'learning by doing' within a 'low skill equilibrium' and based on a relatively itinerant workforce". In sharp contrast, the German construction industry operates a training levy of 2.8% of gross payroll "which all firms in the sector have to pay, regardless of whether or not they train themselves". They argue further that "the greater breadth and depth of German initial training, compared to its UK counterpart, remains the key" to greater German success in adapting to technical changes. German trainees also emerge from their courses not only physically dexterous but also technically knowledgeable and competent. Deep cultural differences are exposed by this comparison – German society offers wide and genuine support for training in general, and for group training centres (to assist firms which do not themselves train) within the construction industry in particular. And yet, as both authors make clear, the construction industry on both sides of the channel faces the same problem of recruiting "a suitably motivated and qualified youth intake", but the German system of training with nationally-recognised qualifications to industry-approved standards responds much more successfully to this shared difficulty.

Further unflattering comparisons emerge from Reiner Siebert's description of Jobrotation, a particularly innovative and cost-neutral measure which enables small and medium firms (SMEs), who cannot afford to be without any of their employees during working hours, to adapt to technical and structural change. Jobrotation, which is currently being tried out in Germany for the first time, was introduced into Denmark more than 10 years ago and now involves 37,000 people annually. The strategy draws heavily on the strong tradition of educational leave in Denmark (currently six weeks per year for all employees) and consists of releasing employees to update their skills, while simultaneously training unemployed people who act as substitutes so that they gain work experience as well as training. The success of this policy initiative (with around one third being kept on by the firm and another third finding jobs elsewhere) has helped to counteract the stereotype of the long-term unemployed. In the midst of his account, Reiner Siebert mentions casually that among the unemployed in Germany (now approaching almost 5 million) "55% hold at least one vocational or HE degree". The implication of this high percentage for policies based solely on increasing the supply of highly qualified workers in the UK is obvious.

The impression given by these first two chapters, however, is that the much praised dual system of vocational training in Germany is not without its problems. British specialists in vocational education have become used to reading about the sclerotic administration and the costly regulations of the German system, but may still be surprised to learn that heavy investment and cultural support for initial vocational training by all the social partners in Germany does not appear to engender a love of lifelong learning. Indeed, Reiner Siebert talks of the dual system as a hindrance to the notion of lifelong learning. If you have received a broad theoretical and practical training which is certified and recognised, then the need for continuous retraining is thereby lessened, as further training means obtaining vocational qualifications to many German skilled workers and *Meister*. Within the *Learning Society Programme*, John Field (1997) and Tom Schuller (1997) are examining the intriguing lack of progression and continuity between achievement in initial education (which is relatively high in both Scotland and Northern Ireland compared with the rest of the UK) and participation in adult education and training which is relatively low in both northern countries.

The second leitmotiv running through this collection of essays deals with competing conceptions of the learning society, and of lifelong learning. Central to these debates are competing definitions of what is to be considered as learning. Isabelle Darmon, Kari Hadjivassiliou, Elliot Stern and other colleagues at the Tavistock Institute argue in Chapter 3 that one particular school of thought within work-based learning, which is curriculum-centred and skills-oriented, holds that "all learning, no matter how acquired, is worthy of recognition and credit". Michael Eraut would not accept this approach and suggests instead that:

> *… the use of the word 'learning' in the phrase 'the learning society' should refer only to significant changes in capability or understanding, and exclude the acquisition of further information when it does not contribute to such changes. One advantage of this definition is that it can be applied at the group, organisational and societal levels as well as that of the individual person. (Eraut, 1997, p 556)*

David Ashton pushes the debate further still in the final chapter by arguing that Michael Eraut's definition of learning leaves out "the changes in attitudes and values, necessary for ensuring the commitment of the individual to both the group and the wider organisation".

A related point made by a number of the contributors is that the national debate about lifelong learning has become dominated by the providers of education and training and this dominance is creating a consequent depreciation of the significance of informal learning. For Michael Eraut and his colleagues, in Chapter 4, "learning from formal education and training … is often of only secondary importance". In the companies studied by David Ashton "training was an infrequent activity but learning was an everyday occurrence".

Adults with learning difficulties constitute a strategically important group for understanding the dominant, utilitarian view of the learning society which prioritises the links between learning and economic success, between qualifications and international competitiveness. The moral question raised by Stephen Baron and his colleagues in Chapter 5 is: are those of us who experience difficulties in learning *allowed* to be members of the learning society? In other words, how would a learning society treat poor learners or non-learners?

This research team wish to see disability interpreted not as a quality of a particular individual but as an active system of "social barriers to full citizenship for people with an impairment". This approach interprets skill, not as an objective and measurable quantity of individuals, but as the result of particular relationships and is well supported in the literature (eg, Collins, 1989). The wide variation in the percentages of the population who attend special schools in Germany (12%) and in the UK (2%) strongly suggests that the concept of disability is differently constructed by different societies. In stressing the case for social justice as well as economic efficiency, this team is also developing a vision of the learning society which articulates "a new combination of utilitarian and humanist discourses, avoiding the weaknesses of both".

The biggest mistake which could be made would be to conclude that we are here dealing with only 3% or 4% of the population who happen to be adults with learning difficulties because, as Manuel Castells argues, the new system of production which he calls informationalism[1] creates "a sharp divide between valuable and non-valuable people and locales" (1998, p 161). He is referring to the processes whereby large and growing numbers of human beings (minorities, immigrants, women, young people and children) become "irrelevant, both as producers and consumers" and fall into the "downward spiral of social exclusion, toward what I have called 'the black holes of informational capitalism'" (pp 344-5). In Castells' bleak vision of the rise of the 'Fourth World', social exclusion and economic irrelevance come to be visited upon not just powerless social groups but upon whole communities, regions, cities and entire countries.

A third recurrent theme in these essays concerns the need for open, trusting relationships among colleagues at work to enable informal learning to thrive. At a basic level, it is obvious that, if workmates do not mix easily and comfortably, they are unlikely to learn much from each other. And yet Peter Scott and Antje Cockrill report in Chapter 1 how within the UK construction industry "an emphasis on competition based on cost minimisation" led to "adversarial low trust relations between contractors themselves and ... between employers and employees".

In contrast, Michael Eraut and his colleagues in Chapter 4 claim that the flattening of hierarchies in many organisations is providing people with the time, space and freedom to develop networks of informal learning. Similarly, in one of David Ashton's case studies, "transforming the company culture involved a basic change in the attitude of management toward the workforce ... the first move ... was to establish a relationship of trust between the company and the unions".

But this is where contradictory policies, being pursued simultaneously within the same firm, transformed learning into a conflictual process. Downsizing and delayering staff, for example, created such tensions in middle managers that they became afraid, according to David Ashton, to pass knowledge and information downwards in case they put their own jobs at risk. In his own words:

> *"... even in organisations which have delayered, hierarchy is still a central feature of everyday experience and has a profound effect on the learning process. Thus it was not uncommon that learning was hindered by bosses who did not trust their subordinates and so were reluctant to share information and knowledge."*

These are some of the structural barriers which organisations themselves erect unwittingly and which prevent individuals and groups from learning as much as they could.

Finally, what is to be learned from these six research reports about the direction of trends in skill formation and what are the immediate implications for policy of these trends? The balance of evidence presented in this volume suggests that, although some firms and industries have not changed significantly, if at all, skill formation is now being increasingly viewed as a continuous process which has moved from the training department to the workplace, and which is more directly geared to improving company performance and meeting business objectives. Furthermore, for David Ashton, skill formation now "encompasses the moulding of attitudes and values as well as the transmission of specific skills".

Such a transformation calls for a corresponding change in the management of learning, from the formal transmission of knowledge and information to the more informal skills of mentoring, coaching and collaborative learning in teams. But many trainers and line managers, whose role has been extended to include responsibility for training, have become accustomed during their careers to the ethos of 'command and control' and so find difficulty in developing the different skills needed to facilitate both the learning of others and the creation of new knowledge. Garvey, Alred and Smith also found in talking to mentors that "they speak as much about the benefits to themselves as about what they feel they have been able to offer to mentees" (1996, p 14). The new training needs of companies in managing the learning process therefore need to be explicitly recognised. As Isabelle Darmon and her colleagues remark in Chapter 3: "the central conundrum of the learning organisation is: if management can be learned, can learning be managed?".

The second implication concerns the importance of informal learning at work and yet most audits of training continue to prioritise formal provision; what is really needed is some integration of informal and formal learning and some more widespread appreciation of the strengths and weaknesses of both. For example, both of the surveys conducted by the National Institute of Adult Continuing Education (NIACE) in 1990 and in 1996 showed that only 15% were studying formally at work (Sargant, 1997, p 48). The work of Michael Eraut and his colleagues underlines the sheer amount of learning from other *people* rather than, say, from manuals or formal training sessions. Their evidence calls for more attention to be paid to the role of the manager as 'staff developer', to the significance of the micro-culture of organisations in supporting or impeding learning, and to the different types of knowledge within firms and how to access them. The increasing importance which researchers are paying to informal learning (see, for instance, Jeffs and Smith, 1997 on the fostering of conversation) runs counter, however, to the national moves to accredit learning formally and to increase the number and level of qualifications held by the workforce.

Thirdly, what comes across from these accounts of the construction industry, and of engineering, business and healthcare firms, is the lack of recognition on the part of management of the

structural barriers which their organisations are unintentionally placing in the path of would-be learners. David Ashton's chapter in particular highlights the conflicts and struggles involved in the process of learning "with the parties involved having different agendas and in many cases not being aware of how to facilitate the process".

The above comments have concentrated on only three themes and a few implications for policy from a very broad range of topics which also include, for example, core competencies and the main issues relating to transfer (in Chapter 3 by Isabelle Darmon and colleagues), discussions of human and social capital (by Stephen Baron et al in Chapter 5) and of standards, credentialism and Modern Apprenticeships and National Vocational Qualifications (in Chapter 1 by Peter Scott and Antje Cockrill). What all six chapters have in common is a realisation that, to make a success of lifelong learning or of a learning society in the UK, much more needs to be known about the key process of *learning* as embedded in particular workplaces, in organisational structures and in specific social practices (see Lave and Wenger, 1991). This report, however, is a serious contribution to achieving that objective and future reports from the *Learning Society Programme* will similarly be dedicated to increasing our understanding still further.

Note

[1] Manuel Castells defines informationalism as "a mode of development in which the main source of productivity is the qualitative capacity to optimise the combination and use of factors of production on the basis of knowledge and information" (1998, p 7).

References

Castells, M. (1998) *End of millennium*, Vol III, Oxford: Blackwell.

Coffield, F. (ed) (1997) *A national strategy for lifelong learning*, Newcastle: Department of Education, Newcastle University.

Collins, H. (1989) *Artificial experts, social knowledge and intelligent machines*, Cambridge, Mass: MIT Press.

Eraut, M. (1997) 'Perspectives on defining "The Learning Society"', *Journal of Education Policy*, vol 12, no 6, November-December, pp 551-8.

Field, J. (1997) 'Northern Ireland – perspectives', in N. Sargant (ed) *The learning divide*, Leicester: NIACE, pp 91-8.

Garvey, B., Alred, G. and Smith, R. (1996) 'First-person mentoring', *Career Development International*, vol 1, no 5, pp 10-14.

Jeffs, T. and Smith, M. (1997) *Informal education: Conversation, democracy and learning*, Derby: Education New Books.

Lave, J. and Wenger, E. (1991) *Situated learning: Legitimate peripheral participation*, Cambridge: Cambridge University Press.

Sargant, N. (1997) *The learning divide,* Leicester: NIACE.

Schuller, T. (1997) 'Scotland – perspectives', in N. Sargant (ed) *The learning divide*, Leicester: NIACE, pp 105.

Artisans in the making? Comparing construction training in Wales and Germany

Peter Scott and Antje Cockrill

Introduction

The construction industry could be justly regarded as a particularly challenging environment within which to uncover evidence of the development of any microcosmic form of learning society. On the one hand, the construction trades have historically been an important route into low skilled employment for less intellectually gifted younger males. In this sense, the industry has fulfilled a social function in providing opportunities to those not suited to less physical environments. And yet, important technological and organisational trends within the industry suggest that it needs increasingly to move away from such a 'low skill' orientation towards one based on higher skill levels and on broader and more extensive training. For example, particularly in the UK, several developments are likely to increase the urgency with which the industry will need to address skills, training and the recombination of occupations. Such trends include: current government-initiated reviews of training provision and of the status of all theoretically 'self-employed' construction workers within the industry; tentative evidence of longer-term, less adversarial relationships between developers, main contractors and sub-contractors in the housebuilding industry (Chevin, 1994), which should lead to greater requirements for team-working, liaison and communication between staff; the adoption of quality assurance and other techniques to improve productivity already tested – and responsibility for enhanced skill levels – in the manufacturing sector (Royal Academy of Engineering, 1996); increased legal and customer pressures for proof of builders' competence; and a technologically-induced evolution towards more complex, generic and intertwined occupational skill requirements (IPRA Ltd, 1992).

This chapter investigates on a cross-national basis the extent of the difficulties inherent in refocusing skills and training in small- and medium-sized enterprises (SMEs) in the Welsh and German construction industries, particularly with respect to any impetus to enhance their existing employees' skill profiles. Our focus is both national, considering the role of established industrial and training structures, and regional, because it is at this more local level of interaction between public administration, enterprises and training institutions that such learning activity is realised. We intend to show how, despite the two countries facing remarkably similar problems with the quality of entrant into the industry, the German system has been rather more successful in furnishing broad transferable skills and a highly inclusive and responsive training infrastructure.

Our data derive from two sources. Firstly, two sets of structured face-to-face interviews were carried out during 1996-97 with SMEs representing a cross-section of construction activity in South Wales in the UK and the German regions of Baden-Württemberg in the South West and Nordrhein-Westfalen in the industrial North West. Interviews were conducted with managers responsible for recruitment, training and development in 25 firms in Wales and 10 in Germany. Our primary concern was the so-called intermediate skill level, within which we include skilled general operatives, the craft trades, and technical and first-line supervisory levels. Information about the firms was supplemented by semi-structured interviews held in each country with the main sectoral organisations representing employers and labour, and also those bodies concerned with the formulation of policy for training in construction and its delivery.

Britain and Germany compared

The comparative performance of the UK building industry relative to its continental counterparts has been disparaged for some time. Ball's assertions (1988, pp 1-2, 7-18) that UK construction suffers more than some foreign building industries from inferior products, management and labour are still mirrored in Clarke and Wall's (1996) more recent conclusions from an Anglo-German-Dutch comparative study of social housebuilding. These and other studies suggest the lagging performance of the British industry is at least partly due to lack of exploitation of technology. This is compounded by skills, training and a workforce that are fragmented in nature and insufficient in quality and adaptability. Numbers of trainees have declined over recent years, levels of workers' certification and take-up of in-service continuing training are both low, the amount of training taking place both in-company and in further education (FE) colleges has fallen (see Scott and Cockrill, 1997, pp 2-4, for more detailed discussion of these points). The qualification structure is increasingly based on National Vocational Qualifications (NVQs), which commentators such as Callender (1992) and Steedman and Hawkins (1994) suggest has led to more restrictively defined trades and less transferability of skill than was previously the case.

Reinforcing these last themes, Clarke (1992) has argued forcefully that recent decades have actually witnessed accelerating forms of disintegration of trades within the construction industry in a number of ways and for various reasons. Among the developments she cites are the rise of new specialist trades due to technological changes, such as increasingly specialised categories of flooring and tiling workers, and the fission of existing crafts. These developments are compounded by the rise of a largely unregulated sub-contracting form of employment relationship, notorious for its aversion to training, but with short-term financial advantages

to those who engage in it. The growth of new fragmented specialisms and of self-employment have together encouraged the expansion of the specialist sub-contracting firm, which further cements the disaggregation of working relationships.

Continental training systems for the construction industry are normally more rigorous, of longer duration, and better resourced than the UK equivalent (see Campinos-Dubernet and Grando, 1988; Further Education Unit, 1992; Prais and Steedman, 1986; Rainbird and Syben, 1991). Skills within the construction industries of Germany and other European nations, and the standards of the qualifications that demonstrate their possession, appear to stand on a more certain grounding than those in the UK. Comparison of the main German apprenticeship qualification, the *Berufsabschluß*, with comparable UK qualifications for the building trades reveals that the former is both broader and deeper and contains greater theoretical and mathematical content (see Steedman, 1992; Steedman and Hawkins, 1994; Steedman, 1996). Moreover, self-employed builders in Germany are better trained and regulated, being required to possess the advanced craft *Meister* qualification before they can set up in business.

Wales

Skills and training in Welsh SMEs

Our findings from SMEs indicate some grounds for optimism as the level of initial trade-based training seems to hold up quite well, although its content is often viewed as having atrophied. Twelve companies (48%) engaged in a programme of initial training (although another five had now ceased offering apprenticeships), with 10 firms participating in the government's Modern Apprenticeship (MA) programme, which was designed to staunch the decline in apprenticeship training in construction. On balance, the firms' evaluation of the progress of MA for them to date was broadly positive. However, the intellectual ability and reliability of apprentices and other recruits were frequently cited as areas of difficulty. Six firms (24%) noted disparagingly that apprentice trainees' motivation was poor, which led to problems such as non-attendance at college and high drop-out rates.

The other main areas of employers' criticism were centred, firstly, upon the view of many that the standards of NVQ-based qualifications were insufficient and, secondly, a perception that the depth of MA compared unfavourably with that of the traditional apprenticeship most of them had undergone. Part of this dissatisfaction related to the current official assumption that three years is sufficient time to produce a rounded craft worker compared to the five years typical of the old 'time-serving' arrangements. Whatever the failings of the old system, many employers were simply unconvinced that a comparable capability would be produced.

More broadly, training occupied a relatively subsidiary role within most of the companies surveyed and few mechanisms are in place for any strategic approach to broadening and deepening the industry's skill base. Five (20%) conceded that it was currently unimportant, while two firms admitted that the importance of training had declined as workloads had diminished; a number of other firms found themselves unable to plan for training due to their overall lack of current work. Training is predominantly viewed reactively: 14 of the SMEs (56%) said that it was primarily geared to meeting, and maintaining awareness of, new legislative and/or safety requirements, such as the Construction (Design and Management) Regulations or the 1991 New Roads and Street Works Act. Yet new quality assurance procedures, notably ISO 9002, had percolated into almost one third (32%) of the companies surveyed, with another three firms currently pursuing the standard, and this had forced a greater formalisation and intensification of training activity in those firms adopting it.

Multiskilling, understood as some degree of cross-trade working, was common: 20 of the firms (80%) claimed that this form of integration of roles was occurring. Yet, formal training for this development was rare indeed, as it has always been within the UK industry. Interview evidence from the Construction Industry Training Board (CITB) suggests that efforts in the late 1960s to foster broader initial training came to little, although it was widely acknowledged that cross-trade working was happening largely unacknowledged and unaccredited in SMEs in particular. In the context of recent developments towards greater modularity and flexibility in

qualifications through the NVQ framework and MA's stated aim to provide broad training, multi-skilling has again aroused some formative interest, yet most of this has come from public sector construction departments and not from the private sector (see ADLO, 1996).

Even so, ADLO's (1996, pp 3, 28) evidence indicates that little or no further *formal* training is being either provided or demanded to enable employees to become multiskilled, and our private sector findings – even from companies that otherwise train actively – amplify this. Many of the case-study firms remained reluctant to allow any official role for multiskilling, mainly because of its suspected adverse effects on costs and ability to realise the economies of scale achievable through trade specialisation. More informally, limited de facto multiskilled working across similar types of trade was occurring especially in firms specialising in repair and maintenance (which, ironically, constitutes just under half of the total value of all UK construction work) and in general builders whose workload was too low to exploit extensive economies of scale. Six firms (24%) considered that workers would be expected to use skills within another trade to a 'do-it-yourself' standard to the extent they felt capable. It was stressed that such cross-skilling rarely, if ever, extended into undertaking electrical work. Sometimes older, more experienced, workers were allocated as 'mentors' to tutor this process of multiskilling, but normally it occurred entirely through an ad hoc process of 'learning by doing'.

SMEs and the training system

A common stereotype exists that construction companies in particular shun contact with outside organisations with responsibilities for training in favour of an isolationist stance underpinned by their existing abilities and resources. In some respects this is true. Most firms find the organisation and funding of construction training complex and confusing, especially concerning the role of Training and Enterprise Councils (TECs). Only seven (28%) of the companies interviewed had any contact with these, and few had found such contact rewarding. Yet few firms appeared to rely exclusively on internal means for training activity. Fifteen of the firms (60%) maintained contact with their industry training organisation, normally the CITB, and only three firms (12%) expressed overt criticism, normally concerned with a perceived lack of support from the body.

There was, however, little evidence of direct inter-firm collaboration to satisfy mutual training needs, although five firms did belong to voluntary regional Construction Industry Training Groups (CITGs), which jointly identified issues and training matters of common local concern, and were to some extent able to organise suitable provision. CITGs exist in each of the former county areas of the South Wales region and are voluntary independent organisations, bringing together representatives of some of the main construction sector employers within each relevant locality, FE colleges, and with administrative support provided by the CITB. Funding is on the basis of payment of a subscription by companies.

Twelve of the firms (48%) used local FE colleges for training purposes and, again, there was remarkably little criticism of their record, although some firms had reservations about the quality, skill levels and attitudes of apprentice trainees FEs supplied. FE colleges themselves were able to provide multi-skilled training and were keen to expand this facility, but remained extremely unsure of likely demand levels from firms, who tended to ask for relatively specific trade-based training.

Germany

Skills and training in German SMEs

Within the German construction industry, the main trend is a 'professionalising' shift towards skilled workers within the overall employment structure and a perception that there is a declining need for the semi-skilled or unskilled. More of the low-skilled tasks are being performed off-site in workshops, and several firms mentioned that they left these tasks to sub-contractors, and performed the skilled tasks with their own workers, who are now required to operate as part of a team able to coordinate and interface with the activities of other contractors on-site. As a consequence of recession, several firms interviewed had stopped taking on new trainees because of the expense of training places and insufficient work to be able to keep them

on. Yet others retained very high proportions of trainees to total employees (1:4 in one case).

Clarke and Wall's (1996) study suggests that the broad-based nature of German construction training focuses its employees more towards the 'industry' as a whole rather than their particular 'trade' or profession. We found some support for this contention, although it may well have been overstated. Indeed, a number of employers interviewed spoke of their difficulty in motivating employees to take on work outside of their immediate occupation and suggested that strong trade-based affinities and demarcations remained. Many German construction firms have been quick to exploit the greater perceived flexibility of skilled foreign construction workers, particularly from former eastern bloc countries, for this very reason, as well as their relative cheapness. On the other hand, there was some, limited, evidence of particular types of contractor working in a more multiskilled way. For instance, skilled workers in two roofing contractors were taking on various additional tasks of other trades in order to be able to inter-mesh satisfactorily with other contractors working on adjoining parts of the structure. As in Britain, there seemed remarkably little evidence that the assumption of such additional skills is accompanied by much formal training, despite the existence of a considerable amount of updating and further training generally in the SMEs visited, often carried out through in-house seminars or inter-company training centres *(überbetriebliche Ausbildungszentren,* described below). A small number of firms had adopted ISO 9002, which was forcing some documentation on training policies and increases in training activity, although other firms remained implacably opposed to the ISO route.

German SMEs and the training system

Training for construction in Germany, strictly speaking, is no longer part of the dual system. Instead, a flexible, hybrid system known as stage training *(Stufenausbildung)* operates in the sector (see also Streeck and Hilbert, 1991). In the late 1960s and early 1970s, it was recognised that the traditional dual system apprenticeship training based on practical training in the company and theoretical education in the vocational school was unsatisfactory, particularly for smaller firms. Costs were a major deterrent to training provision, and the standards and quality of training differed substantially between firms. As in Britain, some young people attracted by the construction sector had relatively low educational attainment.

Legislation was changed and inter-company training centres were introduced in order to address these difficulties. The traditional apprenticeship system was changed to the *Stufenausbildung*. Unlike the dual system, it has three rather than two components: training in the firm, education in the vocational school (*Berufsschule*), and training in the off-site inter-company training centre. Pedagogy in the training centre emphasises the development of what would be called 'key skills' in the UK: teamwork, group work and social skills, all of which are increasingly rare among building apprentices and not taught in the vocational schools. The German solution to maintaining the motivation of possibly less academic trainees was to split the three year apprenticeship into two stages, each leading to an examination for a recognised qualification. The exam concluding the first stage occurs after the second year. This can either be the qualifying exam for the first stage of the full apprenticeship, or it can be taken as the final exam for the qualification as building worker. The second stage, in the third year, for the full apprenticeship leads to exams for skilled worker status in a specific craft.

In the first year of their apprenticeship, trainees only spend a very limited amount of time in the firm (12 weeks). This is complemented by 20 weeks in the vocational school and 20 weeks in the inter-company training centre. The training in the first year focuses on general introductory training in all building trades. In the second year, the trainee spends 26 weeks in the firm, and 13 each in the training centre and vocational school. At this stage, trainees follow one of three broad training paths: building, finishing, or civil engineering trades. Finally, in the third year, this balance changes completely, and most of the time is spent in the firm, and only eight and four weeks are spent in the vocational school and the training centre respectively. In the third year, the trainee finally specialises in just one of the currently available 16 construction trades or crafts, each of which is rather broader than its nearest UK equivalent.

Funding mechanisms have also been changed. Training in the construction sector is now funded via a training levy, which all firms in the sector have to pay, regardless of whether or not they train themselves. Presently they have to contribute 2.8% of their gross payroll. These funds are used to reimburse firms for trainees' allowances during the time they spent in the training centre. This system was introduced to balance the costs of training and non-training firms, and thus to discourage non-training firms from poaching other firms' trainees. Training centres also conduct a lot of further and continuing training, much of it leading to externally recognised qualifications, such as the *Meister* award, and also courses in renovation, environmental and fire protection, management skills and business administration, and so on.

In Germany, provision and funding for construction industry training has been more stable than in the UK, despite the need for a relatively high degree of input from employers because of the additional levy for stage training. Yet this is relatively uncontroversial. Overall, widespread consensus remained within the German firms for the principles of the *Stufenausbildung* system, its broad-based practical training, emphasis on developing transferable skills, and its ability to unite theory and practice. All our respondents considered the inter-company training centres to be important and successful, and reported positive experiences with them, usually based upon close, interactive working relationships with the *Meister* at the local *Ausbildungszentrum*. There was a general consensus that such centres could provide more uniform standards of initial training than firms could, and that training could be provided which would go beyond the means of any individual company. A minority of employers remained concerned that some of the practical grounding provided in all building trades was unnecessary, as in the case of one specialist plastering firm which questioned whether its trainees really needed to learn how to build roads and pavements.

However, opinions about the role and functioning of the *Berufsschulen* vocational schools within the traineeship were considerably more sceptical. Many employers felt that apprentices spent too much time in the vocational school (especially in the first year), and that this time was poorly used. They disliked the requirement that apprentices participated in general subjects such as religion and physical education, and to a lesser extent, in English and German lessons. Other areas of criticism we encountered concerned the number of lessons cancelled due to lack of teachers, a lack of contact and cooperation between firms and vocational schools except during emergencies or at times when something went wrong, and insufficient preparation of apprentices for the final qualifying examination. Despite the many complaints about vocational schools, employers still seemed to retain a consensus that their general principle was correct, that some theory and general knowledge was desirable for apprentices, and that this could not be provided in the firm. However, there was also almost universal agreement that the present format of this training element worked poorly for both training firms and apprentices themselves.

As in Britain, the German employers traced a considerable part of these problems with the schools back to the low initial calibre of apprentices themselves: absenteeism, lack of motivation and poor initial qualifications contributed to uneasy relations between schools, trainees and firms, which are compounded when schools must work with very large numbers of employers with differing needs. Many employers argued that the German construction industry ends up performing a social function for the less qualified and motivated youth intake, many of whom are non-native Germans and face greater social problems than average. Considerable difficulties were encountered in finding a sufficient quantity of workers and, even more so, trainees of suitable quality in terms of attitude, ability and motivation to fill apprenticeship places.

Construction SMEs and the learning society

One can exaggerate the differences between UK and German industry. In the case of construction, we saw above that both countries face similar difficulties in attracting a suitably motivated and qualified youth intake (tackled in Germany through providing two different formal levels of apprentice qualification in the *Stufenausbildung*). Even in

Germany, elements remain of lack of willingness or ambition to venture beyond the boundaries of existing trades and occupations, which limits the effectiveness of strategic moves towards multiskilling and, although it does occur widely on an unspoken and ad hoc basis, relatively little formal training is ever provided for it.

On the other hand, the German construction industry operates from a higher and more secure base-line than its UK equivalent. The greater breadth and depth of the German initial training compared to its UK counterpart remains the key to what appears to constitute better German success in absorbing and adapting to subsequent technical and organisational change affecting construction trades. The German system also functions within a network of high-trust relationships. The relatively broad craft basis on which the division of labour pivots is not questioned as a basis for future development, although there might well be scope to continue the process of eliminating demarcations through a more proactive policy of multiskilling. However, demand for this is not widespread at the level of the firm. Despite the reservations about the role of the vocational schools within the training system, the stage training method is widely and genuinely supported. The synergy of construction SMEs and inter-company training centres in particular has enabled the fruition of a form of interactive learning and responsive further training provision at local level which has deep roots because of the inclusive constituency of the *Ausbildungszentren*. This is particularly important in view of the relatively higher technology methods utilised by the German industry, which arguably imply greater recourse to a need for rapid updating than many UK methods.

By contrast, much of the UK industry clings grimly to an informal mode of poorly accredited 'learning by doing' within a 'low skill equilibrium' and based on a relatively itinerant workforce. Skill bases are transparent only within the extended local labour markets upon which so many firms rely as a defence against the uncertain quality of recruit furnished by a haphazard formal provision of training, although MA may help remedy this. The penchants for opaque methods of skill formation and proof are coupled with an emphasis on competition based on cost minimisation, leading to adversarial low trust relations between contractors themselves and, moreover, similar confrontation between employers and employees. The dominance of the drive to reduce contractors' risk within the construction process, especially that element engendered by dependence on the construction labour force, has favoured the expansion of self-employment and the fragmentation of the craft trades. The extent of the fragmentation pursued now endangers any ready ability to recombine skills, even though this might often only restore the former formal content of some trades and legitimate what appears to occur largely unofficially in some sub-sectors of the industry anyway. Cost implications are likely to be a further barrier unless decisive sectors of the industry continue to distance themselves from Taylorist strategies. Luckily, factors such as the anticipated boost to the proportion of directly employed labour and the enhanced role for quality assurance may enable more inclusive human resource strategies to gain added strength, at least in the medium-sized and more forward-looking companies.

A similar reluctance by many SMEs to engage with the training system that is viewed as externally designed and imposed hinders the revival of initial training, further development, and the formal development of more broadly skilled workers in a manner that is of any practical use beyond the boundaries of the individual firm. The unwillingness arises partly from the resilience of the voluntarist tradition of informal training and more traditional ideas of apprenticeship that exert a more active influence over practices in construction than perhaps in any other sector. However, there is also both suspicion and sheer confusion about a system whose partitioning of responsibilities and succession of externally developed initiatives appears complex to the average construction firm. In Germany the divisions of roles and responsibilities for teaching and funding are well understood and accepted, as are the standards that trainees are expected to reach. In the UK, the frictional and competitive (or at least non-communicative) relationships within the training system between largely college-based providers, policy makers, and funders are not, and our research suggests that the issue of standards needs addressing urgently. Examples of collaborative learning by interaction between colleges and firms do exist, but are far more embryonic than the more embedded apparatus facilitated in Germany by inter-company

training centres. The CITGs described in Wales bring together the CITB, colleges and construction firms, but their membership remains entirely voluntary on the part of firms and thus risks having any appreciable impact only on the practices of what one suspects is a minority of firms already sufficiently motivated and 'converted'. It seems unlikely, given the insularity of much of the UK construction sector, that change can successfully be imposed from the outside. And, though some SMEs seem to view the admittedly poor state of skills and training with complacency or resignation, we can only hope that the momentum of the lobby for increased qualification, professionalism and skill levels emanating from major sources within the industry will carry enough of the UK industry successfully in its wake.

Authors' acknowledgements

This chapter is prepared from findings out of the Centre for Advanced Studies/School of Education project at University of Wales Cardiff under the *Learning Society Programme* (ESRC grant no L123251020). The Cardiff project director is Professor Phil Cooke, supported by Dr John Fitz and Professor Brian Davies. We are grateful to all the respondents who gave freely of their time in interviews in Germany and Wales. We would also like to acknowledge the useful comments of the participants at the Learning Society Initiative meeting on skill formation, University of Bristol, 27-28 May 1997.

References

ADLO (Association of Direct Labour Organisations) (1996) *Building trade multi-skilling: Training requirements of construction work and building maintenance DLOs*, Manchester: ADLO.

Ball, M. (1988) *Rebuilding construction*, London: Routledge.

Callender, C. (1992) *Will National Vocational Qualifications work? Evidence from the construction industry*, IMS Report No 228, Brighton: Institute of Manpower Studies.

Campinos-Dubernet, M. and Grando, J.-M. (1988) 'Formation Professionelle Ouvrière: Trois Modèles Européens', *Formation/Emploi*, no 22, pp 5-29.

Chevin, D. (1994) 'Terms of endearment', *Building*, 2 December, pp 18-9.

Clarke, L. (1992) *The building labour process: Problems of skills, training and employment in the British construction industry in the 1980s*, Occasional Paper 50, Ascot: Chartered Institute of Building.

Clarke, L. and Wall, C. (1996) *Skills and the construction process: A comparative study of vocational training and quality in social housebuilding*, Bristol: The Policy Press.

Further Education Unit (1992) *Vocational education and training in Europe: A four-country study in four employment sectors*, London: Further Education Unit.

IPRA Ltd (1992) *Future skill needs of the construction industries*, Brighton: IPRA Ltd.

Prais, S.J. and Steedman, H. (1986) 'Vocational training in France and Britain: the building trades', *National Institute Economic Review*, no 116, pp 45-55.

Rainbird, H. and Syben, G. (eds) (1991) *Restructuring a traditional industry: Construction employment and skills in Europe*, Oxford: Berg.

Royal Academy of Engineering (1996) *A statement on the construction industry*, London: Royal Academy of Engineering.

Scott, P. and Cockrill, A. (1997) *Skills and training in the construction industry: The UK experience and lessons from Germany*, ESRC Learning Society Initiative Project Working Paper No 6, Cardiff: CASS/School of Education, University of Wales Cardiff.

Steedman, H. (1992) *Mathematics in vocational youth training for the building trades in Britain, France and Germany*, NIESR Discussion Papers No 9, London: National Institute for Economic and Social Research.

Steedman, H. (1996) 'The German *Berufabschluss* qualification: What do German apprentices learn?', paper to University of Westminster workshop on 'Skills and the Construction Process', 17 May, London: Centre for Economic Performance, London School of Economics.

Steedman, H. and Hawkins, J. (1994) 'Shifting foundations: the impact of NVQs on youth training for the building trades', *National Institute Economic Review*, no 149, August, pp 93-102.

Streeck, W. and Hilbert, J. (1991) 'Organised interests and vocational training in the West German construction industry', in H. Rainbird and G. Syben (eds) *Restructuring a traditional industry: Construction employment and skills in Europe*, Oxford: Berg, pp 241-60.

Jobrotation: combining skills formation and active labour market policy

Reiner Siebert

Introduction

Promoting educational leave schemes is one approach which allows employees to upgrade their work-related skills and knowledge and which introduces unemployed substitutes at the temporarily vacant workplaces. This is the basic idea of an international project called *Jobrotation*, currently carried out in 14 countries of the European Union (EU).

The term 'jobrotation' originates from a personnel and quality management concept. The idea is quite simple: to prevent burn-out, bureaucratic routines and resistance to change by rotating employees and jobs within the company. Employees will develop new ideas, will be inspired, improve cross-departmental cooperation and understanding and upgrade their skills and experience internally. Obviously, shifting people around creates problems for hierarchies, competences, salaries, and status, etc. However, there are companies still very keen on it. The European headquarters of Fuji (photo and film equipment) near Eindhoven, The Netherlands, is just one example of a multinational company using jobrotation as a major long-term instrument to improve flexibility and create dynamic interaction within its workforce.

The concept to be discussed here is also called jobrotation, probably because it also involves a certain (temporary) mobility and exchange of activities and jobs, but also a form of mobility of people and businesses in terms of education and innovation. However, jobrotation as we see it goes far beyond the entrepreneurial management of personnel. It aims at nothing less than opening access to a continuing learning process for employees while taking into account that the initiation of such a process has profound effects on the organisation of work itself. This, in turn, brings in the employment aspect of jobrotation as an additional goal: combined with the promotion of continuing and further vocational education, jobrotation seeks to offer new employment opportunities for those unemployed who find it difficult to escape the vicious circle of unemployment, government schemes and the lack of on-the-job experience.

In the following sections we shall give an overview of the jobrotation concept and the project *Jobrotation NRW* currently running in the German state of North Rhine Westphalia within a network comprising more than 30 partners in 14 countries of the EU. The employment and labour market aspect of jobrotation will be the main focus, particularly attitudes towards the (re-)transition from unemployment to regular employment. Finally, the educational side of jobrotation will be highlighted, and the reactions and expectations of employees are viewed in the context of the needs and demands of skill formation in small and medium-sized enterprises (SMEs).

This report summarises experiences and conclusions drawn so far from numerous contacts with key persons from enterprises, unions and trade associations, politicians and officials from ministries, labour and social affairs offices, and journalists as well as employees and jobseekers. However, jobrotation is not an academic research project but a practical way of testing, organising, preparing and funding the jobrotation concept. Research in the form of continuous documentation and evaluation of the implementation process is, therefore, descriptive rather than analytical or representative. The sample, which consists of some 300 employees and unemployed people as well as key persons from public and private institutions and companies, is drawn according to availability and fundability rather than to academic standards.[1]

The jobrotation concept

Jobrotation has been tested and implemented in Denmark for 10 years and is one of a number of active Danish labour market policies. A widely recognised tool today, it involves some 37,000 employed and unemployed participants annually. The idea has primarily been regarded as one way of easing the problem of long-term unemployment, and it basically promotes temporary work schemes of a new kind: bottlenecks created by employees' temporary leave are avoided by periods of subsidised employment. So, jobrotation has two major roots: firstly, it tries to enable employees to leave their jobs temporarily because of maternity, paternity, or sabbatical periods or for education without reducing their regular income and without creating bottlenecks at their place of work. Secondly, unemployed people, acting as substitutes, are given the chance to be trained and qualified according to market needs and to gain on-the-job work experience and connections.

While the concept generally allows substitution periods for any kind of leave, the projects which are being run within the EU-Jobrotation network primarily concentrate on the promotion of educational leave in SMEs. These projects have been launched to evaluate the implementation of the jobrotation concept within a particular legal and structural framework. Funded under the EU community initiative ADAPT as part of the European Social Fund, the projects address SMEs trying to adapt to technological and structural change. A continuing process of information, exchange and evaluation among the partners helps to promote mutual understanding of cultural and political differences with the general aim of creating transnational comparison and overall instruments flexible enough to be adapted nationally. Thus,

jobrotation could become a common European approach integrated in the EU-Commission's employment policies and initiatives, the importance of which were reconfirmed at the EU summit in Amsterdam in June 1997 and the Employment Summit in Luxemburg in November 1997.

Jobrotation draws its innovative character from the fact that it combines aspects of education, economic, employment and labour market policies based on the assumption that none of these fields of policy can individually provide solutions to the problems facing the industrialised societies of the 1990s. Unemployment, technological development, the information society and, consequently, continuous processes of learning and adapting, education and training are the major challenges at the turn of the century. Jobrotation is one approach to meet these challenges on an interdisciplinary level.

Jobrotation NRW as a pilot project in North Rhine Westphalia will last for three years with a project budget of some eight million German marks (GM) (£2.7m). Set in a region with 18 million inhabitants with the Rhine-Ruhr conurbation at its centre, the project is of particular importance in an area formerly dominated by heavy industries. Re-development activities of various kinds have been undertaken since the 1960s, but although the economic landscape of the region has changed significantly, big multinational steel companies like Mannesmann, Thyssen or Krupp, still play a prominent role. However, further diversification and a strong trend towards services are visible. Since 1961 the share of the secondary sector in GDP has been reduced from 52% to less than 40%, while the tertiary sector has grown from 46% to 59%. Similarly, in terms of employment the secondary sector has lost almost one million jobs, now accounting for some 40% of all jobs, whereas the tertiary sector now provides almost 60% of all jobs in the region. Today there are more than 600,000 SMEs in the region whose annual turnover amounts to some GM140billion (£50bn).

As in other industrialised countries, these companies are thought to play a crucial role in creating and maintaining economic development and employment. Yet, this means that vocational education and training systems in general and the provision of continuous further training in particular need to be adapted to the special situation of SMEs, which are particularly vulnerable in times of changing markets and growing (international) competition since they can neither rely on considerable capital stocks nor on relatively stable market shares. Still, the necessity to keep up with technological and organisational change is as high as it is for bigger companies. But while larger organisations can cover this need at least partly by maintaining their own research and training departments, SMEs depend heavily on the external provision of training.

SMEs find it hard to plan their activities over a long period of time. Flexibility and tailor-made solutions are their key advantages in markets which require a highly flexible workforce. Each employee is permanently needed and expected to be continuously present. SMEs cannot afford to keep constantly the maximum number of employees needed at production peaks. Rather they tend to keep this number as close to the minimum as possible, covering peaks mainly by working overtime, which, in turn, creates the risk that companies might manage without training altogether because they cannot do without any of their employees during working hours. Consequently, it is often up to employees to upgrade their skills and knowledge in night classes. Very few SMEs do what seems to be of crucial importance: creating medium- and long-term development plans which include the further qualification of personnel.

Jobrotation offers a way out of this difficulty by providing funds for further training courses for employees during working hours and by providing skilled and suitable substitutes to fill the vacant workplaces. While the companies grant their employees educational leave without reducing their income, the jobseekers temporarily employed as substitutes are provided free of charge in order to increase the incentive for employees to undertake vocational training. The substitutes are financed by the respective local labour offices or the communal social services offices which maintain their unemployment benefit or income support during the substitution period.

Jobrotation and employment policy

Despite all the political promises and programmes, training schemes and short-term initiatives to deal with unemployment, nevertheless, it seems to have become a common feature of societies. The phenomenon that large and growing numbers of people, officially registered or not, do not temporarily or ever succeed in making their living and a considerable part of their social interaction through some kind of economic activity, employed or self-employed, has, in fact, created a new, very heterogeneous structure within society. Looking at society on the basis of apparent class divisions will not be of more than cultural and historical significance.

When dealing with initiatives and projects intended to have an impact on unemployment, one must first of all be aware of their limitations. This is as true for jobrotation as for any other measure. One major problem all vocational training schemes, placement or job practice initiatives have in common is that they cannot directly create jobs (apart from those for the trainers and project managers). They are based on the assumption that it is necessary to make individuals competitive on the labour market and to keep the currently inactive part of the labour force updated for expected medium and long-term demands created by economic growth. This approach does, of course, run the risk that competition levels in terms of skills and qualification keep rising which leaves those who are – for whatever reasons - excluded from participation in training schemes even more marginalised than before.

The fact that many jobseekers lack on-the-job experience at work was expected to be the major hindrance to the (re-)transition from unemployment to employment. Consequently, the provision of work practice was believed to be sufficient incentive for the unemployed to take an interest in the project. Unexpectedly, experience so far has shown that it is not enough just to offer work to the unemployed and free substitution to the employers.

Although the idea of jobrotation has generally been well received, negotiations with company managers and owners have revealed widespread scepticism about state-run projects on the one hand and the labour offices' ability to provide qualified and motivated employees on the other. Various SMEs have been ready to take on new employees and create new jobs but did not receive suitable candidates from the labour offices. This is an astonishing fact bearing in mind that there are 4½ million officially registered unemployed and another estimated 2 million jobseekers in Germany.

So, providing qualified substitutes to the companies has been found to be of even higher importance to the introduction and development of jobrotation schemes than the provision of funds. Therefore, the recruitment of suitable candidates for substitution has been granted high priority in the project. Within the first nine months of the project, intensive negotiations and investigations have been held on the macro and micro levels in order to find applicable schemes for finance and methods for recruitment. Close cooperation with the central and local labour offices and the local authority social services offices in and outside North Rhine-Westphalia has been established. Several databases and job banks of these institutions as well as vocational training institutions were used to find substitutes and to promote the jobrotation idea among the unemployed.

However, the specific characteristics of the unemployed population and labour market policy in Germany have had a considerable impact on the design of jobrotation pilot projects. Firstly, due to the well established dual system of initial vocational training in Germany, the proportion of skilled workers among the unemployed is relatively high. More than 55% of all registered unemployed in Germany hold at least one vocational or higher education degree. In addition to this, one of the central parts of German active labour market policy is the provision of further vocational training and retraining to the unemployed. Despite serious cuts in the federal budget, the Federal Labour Office spent GM21.4billion (more than £7bn) on vocational training schemes in 1995.

As a result, it has hardly been necessary so far to design jobrotation pilots including external vocational training periods as preparation for substitutes, which, however, does not necessarily mean that it is easy to find suitable substitutes. The

problem we are facing is how to make ends meet, that is, *Jobrotation NRW* has mainly had to act as an intermediary bringing unemployed and project companies together. Indeed, most unemployed who are suitable for and interested in substitution do not lack vocational skills but on-the-job work experience. On the one hand, it has become obvious that job offers and application procedures by the companies and placement activities of labour offices as traditional ways of bringing jobseekers into employment very often do not lead to successful placements. Companies are very easily discouraged if they fail to find the right person for a job, while, on the other hand, many of the unemployed tend to give up looking for a job altogether and try to obtain access to new, promising vocational retraining although, in fact, they do not lack skills but practice.

Although unemployed people are often trapped in the vicious circle of unemployment and government schemes, it cannot be taken for granted that they are prepared to work on unemployment benefit. After giving up their job search and often with little chance of acceptance onto any other vocational training scheme, many of them have accepted that they will receive unemployment benefit or income support for a long period of time. They have organised their lives around this, doing an odd job here and there. So, they are only willing to act as substitutes, if they see a promising, positive opportunity for themselves. Scepticism about being exploited or put on another dead-end scheme is widespread. As the unemployment benefit or income support is sometimes too low to allow a person an active participation in working life, the willingness to get on full-time substitution while giving up private arrangements tends to be very low. However, the first pilots have shown some promising results: as stated above, many companies do not consider the financial efforts of finding suitable substitutes as problematic. In two of the pilots so far, the companies agreed to give additional financial support to the substitutes, which, in turn, has created problems with the respective labour offices, as additional income on top of unemployment benefit is only allowed at very low levels. Intensive investigation and negotiations have led to solving the problem with yet another path through the jungle of labour market bureaucracy open for future projects.

This bureaucratic side of the implementation process has turned out to be more problematic than previously expected. Substitutes receive unemployment benefit and/or income support on the basis of national legislation. While unemployment benefit is granted by the labour offices in relation to previous income, income support is paid by the local authorities up to a certain maximum according to the needs of the particular family. Placing an unemployed person as a substitute in a company while maintaining unemployment benefit or income support requires that he or she is registered in a scheme allowing on-the-job placement in accordance with the respective legislation. This has been rather complicated to comply with as it has not only meant an in-depth analysis of the legal framework in order to find suitable schemes and support of the high level representatives. Additionally, it has been necessary to negotiate the placement of each substitute with the respective (autonomous) local labour or social affairs offices. So, even with a suitable unemployed person willing to work as substitute, successful jobrotation pilots often depend on the individual willingness of a local officer. However, the jobrotation pilots that have been started so far have ended positively with cooperation between labour and social affairs offices despite the – sometimes – long and tiring discussions and bureaucratic procedures.

For the project as a whole, various sources for the recruitment of substitutes have been located. Apart from the labour offices and the social affairs offices which will always act as the funding body in jobrotation projects for the substitutes' training, on-the-job training and placement, a number of educational organisations have been contacted in order to find substitutes in running schemes who could be placed during practice periods. In some cases the substitutes might be funded through European Social Fund grant training schemes, but this is rather exceptional.

Jobrotation and vocational education

Jobrotation NRW was originally projected to involve a minimum of 180 employees and 100 substitutes.

This projection was made assuming that 100% of the costs for training employees would be covered by project funds. All but one of the rotation agreements concluded so far have caused a revision of this projection. Unexpectedly, the vast majority of companies are prepared to contribute to their employees' training costs. As a result, the standard funding rate for this has been reduced to an average 50%, which implies that more employees will be able to benefit from project funds.

As far as the contents of the training courses for the employees are concerned, the majority of the companies and the employees themselves have very clear ideas about what knowledge and skills should be upgraded and who should go on training. The notion that due to the tailor-made approach whereby each pilot can be organised, run, and specifically adapted to company needs has been received very positively. So, apart from getting the pilots started, this has contributed to the promotion and appreciation of jobrotation.

The vast majority of training courses for the employees are short-term (up to three months) mainly dealing with technology-based skills and knowledge, whereas soft skills have been largely under-represented. These experiences suggest that the necessity to provide training to upgrade employees' soft skills like flexibility, mobility or communication skills, which is often claimed by analysts and researchers, rather applies to the departmental structure of big companies where, traditionally, employees have been expected to specialise. In SMEs, on the other hand, these soft skills have been part of the inner-company socialisation process and on-the-job experience, whereas there is a constant and visible need to keep up with technological developments. Consequently, soft skills are less likely to be covered by external training but more likely to be expected from applicants and newcomers. For jobrotation this means that training in soft skills seems to be much more important for substitutes than for employees of SMEs, which also require a thorough and well-prepared assessment and selection procedure going far beyond the standard placement tests and job interviews.

The efforts to promote the further training of employees undertaken during the implementation process have revealed two major problems so far: firstly, companies are not prepared to provide or allow training when they cannot forsee its effects, and, secondly, further training is less likely to be performed when it depends on the initiative of the employees themselves.

The general upgrading of skills, soft skills and also training periods of more than three months are hard to put into practice. Even if employers generally agree to the importance of such skills, they turn out to be very reluctant when it comes to choosing the employees and the courses. Training is generally supported according to very specific and sometimes urgent company needs like the introduction of new machinery or new technological standards. In these cases the initiative almost always comes from the management itself and is widely supported by the respective employees chosen for the training course as they see it as another or new career opportunity. Accordingly, some of the problems expected to occur in jobrotation projects do not apply in these cases. It had been expected that employees might be worried about being compared with the substitutes, who could eventually do their jobs better. This has not been the case so far as the employees expected to get better working conditions and higher responsibility after the training. Similarly, employers have not expressed considerable worry about employees leaving the company for a better job afterwards, possibly also because of the currently very tight labour market. So, jobrotation has proved to be a very effective tool for vocational training directly related to very specific company needs which the employers or the management themselves found to be obvious but could not cover because of the constant work load.

As far as the employees' initiative to undertake further training is concerned, the project has found two trends. Those employees who are interested in the acquisition of new or updated skills to improve their own position in the labour market or to be better at their jobs, face considerable reluctance from employers to carry out the training during working hours, even if the courses might eventually turn out to be positive for the company itself.

Surprisingly, there are also many employees who do not show any pronounced interest in further training at all. A lot of these are skilled workers and

highly qualified employees who seem automatically to combine further vocational training with the acquisition of vocational qualification certificates, which they do not consider necessary for themselves anymore. This astonishing attitude suggests that a firmly established system of national vocational qualifications, which the German dual system of vocational training has provided for many years, and all German vocational retraining schemes are based on, could turn out to be counterproductive. In Germany acquiring such a certificate is often seen as the termination of a learning process, a notion the term *Beruf* as a vocational occupation for life supports. The notion of national vocational qualifications as the basis and entry to a process of lifelong learning has seemingly not yet received widespread support.

Conclusion

Jobrotation as a new concept of combining aspects of employment, education and economic policies certainly has the potential to open new ways to initiate and support a process of lifelong learning and to offer new employment opportunities for the unemployed. The mid-term experiences and results of the project *Jobrotation NRW*, as described above, have shown widespread interest and support for the idea. The prospects for the introduction of jobrotation as a regular instrument of labour market policy appear to be very promising, although a number of changes to legislation will have to be made in order to reduce the disabling effects of bureaucratic procedures.

New ways of getting the unemployed into companies and providing the companies with qualified employees seem to be needed. The fact that many companies in the sample who expressed profound interest in taking on new staff but could not find or be provided with suitable candidates suggests an urgent need for a revision of application and placement strategies which the companies themselves cannot afford.

The objective that jobrotation might help the initiation of lifelong learning processes and continuous vocational training has not yet been fulfilled in a satisfying way. Neither companies nor employees seem to be fully prepared yet to devote themselves to continuous learning apart from updating the skills which are urgently needed. In this respect jobrotation has at least been able to provide support.

The particular situation of SMEs in the way they organise their work and compete in markets will have to be examined more thoroughly to adapt education and employment policies to their specific needs. The introduction of educational leave systems seems to be one way to encourage continuous learning, and, with the help of jobrotation, to give the unemployed new chances to demonstrate their abilities in the job. We are convinced that the idea will catch on and provide new opportunities for both the employed and unemployed.

Note

[1] As Jobrotation is an implementation project, and this report is based on experiences of implementation, we have not used any literature to form a theoretical basis of this report. We have therefore not used quotes. The figures are taken from official statistics of the State of North Rhine Westphalia, the Federal Republic of Germany and internal papers of the EU-Jobrotation network.

3

Continuing vocational training: key issues

Isabelle Darmon, Kari Hadjivassiliou, Elisabeth Sommerlad, Elliot Stern, Jill Turbin with Dominique Danau

Introduction

This chapter is based on the literature review undertaken for the Economic and Social Research Council (ESRC)-funded project 'Innovation in continuing vocational training (CVT) in the workplace: A comparative perspective'. This project is part of the ESRC *Learning Society Programme*. The chapter discusses the main issues that have emerged from the existing body of literature relevant to work-based learning (WBL), innovations in CVT, vocational education and training systems and transferability.

Work-based learning and continuing vocational training[1]

The following section deals with issues related to the emergence of WBL and CVT as key levers in the quest for competitive advantage, as well as the provision of CVT at company level. It also discusses developments in the area of core competences and the concept of the 'learning organisation'.

Why have WBL and CVT become important?

A number of developments have elevated the importance of WBL and CVT, making them central to the discourse of education and training. These include new social and economic arrangements, such as the move of industrialised nations towards a more knowledge-intensive economy, relying less on the manufacture of labour-intensive mass products

(increasingly moving to the much cheaper labour markets of the third world) and more on the production of high-quality products and services requiring a knowledge input. In addition, the increased globalisation and interdependency of national economies, helped by the gradual and worldwide removal of trade barriers and the lowering of transportation costs, have created a global structure of economic competition.

In such a global market, geographical shifts in the spatial organisation of capital, that is, the establishment, expansion or closure of enterprises, are primarily based on economic cost advantage, compelling a shift of labour-intensive industries to countries that have a considerably lower wage level. In the advanced industrialised nations, the ability of organisations to remain competitive increasingly depends on the effectiveness by which organisations innovate their products, services and processes.

In addition, demographic changes are contributing to renewed interest in WBL and CVT. Specifically, in many industrialised nations, the inflow of new entrants to the labour market is decreasing and this trend is expected to continue. Over 80% of the year 2000's workforce is already in the labour market, while the annual entry of young people into the labour market accounts for only 2% of the active workforce (Cassels, 1990, p 27). At both the macro/government policy and the micro/enterprise levels, this means that many future skill requirements will have to be met by training and retraining current employees rather than by recruiting and training young people. As a result, adult education, lifelong learning and CVT as an ongoing development of skills have acquired a new significance.

At company level, there has been a qualitative shift in production methods in the advanced industrialised countries, uneven in both time and space. This has been popularised as a shift from Fordist techniques of mass production, characterised by semi-skilled work on an assembly line, to post-Fordist production, with multiskilled workers producing a more diversified range of products with shorter product life cycles[2]. Much routine assembly work has been automated, leading to large-scale redundancies but requiring a higher level of skills[3] and attitudinal change on the part of the remaining workforce. Murray has summed up these new working methods as involving:

> *... a core of multiskilled workers whose tasks include not only manufacture and maintenance, but the improvement of the products and processes under their control.... In post-Fordism the worker is designed to act as a computer as well as a machine. (Murray, 1991, p 63)*

This shift has been accompanied by increasing specialisation in product market niches as well as by changes in the distribution of workplaces, that is, a move towards small-scale units of production of both products and services, often linked through customer–supplier relationships. In addition, the strong pressure towards better quality and shorter life cycles of products and services strengthens the need to develop more integrated strategies for new technology, work organisation and skill formation. In this respect, the Tayloristic principle of work organisation often tends to be too rigid to meet the new market demands for quality and flexibility. Instead, principles like teamwork, flatter hierarchies, decentralisation of control and responsibility are rapidly evolving with clear implications for both WBL and CVT.

The general trend is that organisations have to become more flexible, add more value to their products and services and consider the capacities within the organisation as a source for competitive advantage (Danau and Sommerlad, 1996). In fact, contemporary theorisation on organisations holds that knowledge-building is the key source of advantage in the post-industrial era[4]. The debate on organisational learning and the 'learning organisation' which has become prominent in recent years has added further currency to the argument that the survival and competitiveness of organisations are dependent on the competences and commitment of their members and in particular their ability to anticipate change, adapt to new circumstances and come up with new solutions and ideas regarding products and processes.

Despite the prominence given to education and training in current debates, there is a considerable unevenness in the participation of individuals in learning and training activities. It has been long established that certain 'broad' groupings are under-represented in learning and training. These groups have been identifiable by characteristics such as age, gender, ethnicity, socioeconomic background, school-leaving age, previous participation in training, employment status, type of work, income, marital status and domestic responsibilities. In terms of employees engaging in training, it has been shown that participation is low among workers who are: in part-time, seasonal or casual jobs (peripheral workforce[5]); self-employed; employed in small and medium-sized enterprises (SMEs); unskilled; and those lacking educational qualifications.

What are the main theoretical underpinnings?

While there is a seemingly wide consensus about the workplace as a key resource for learning, there are diverse conceptions about what constitutes learning and the workplace. The field of WBL is characterised by overlapping and competing paradigms at the level of both theory and practice. What unites WBL is its pragmatic or instrumental focus; what it lacks, however, is a theoretical drive (beyond the many different learning theories on which it draws). In consequence incongruities and contradictions permeate WBL. Social actors use the different terms to make competing claims for the use of public and private resources across a broad spectrum of development activities.

In broad terms, WBL is facing two directions (Danau and Sommerlad, 1996, p 33). As Danau and Sommerlad note, one is the direction of the VET system, where the interest in the articulation between the world of education and the world of work is primarily conceived within the curriculum-centred, skills-oriented framework of VET. The main thrust of developments within this orientation is the idea, that *all learning, no matter how acquired, is worthy of recognition and credit*. The discourse of researchers and practitioners is centred on skills, competences, learning outcomes and transferable skills. This approach relies primarily on behaviourism and cognitive theories of learning that are highly individualistic and atomistic.

The other direction is the workplace as a learning environment where learning is understood as a process embedded in production and organisational structures (see Cibbora and Schneider, 1992). Learning is about participation in communities of practice, becoming engaged in socially organised activities and so about membership and construction of diverse bonds with other participants. Here the discourse of researchers, theorists and practitioners is centred on learning processes, organisational capability, core competences, knowledge creation and social identity. The main theories it draws from are functionalist, contextual, socio-historical and anthropological which view learning as a collective activity taking place in individuals, but also in social aggregates such as teams, subdivisions of the organisation, the organisation itself, and even the communities within which the organisation interacts.

Finally, there is middle ground in WBL occupied by those researchers and practitioners who seek to establish the common ground between these two orientations or to bridge the gap between them. In this case, the main focus is on the kinds of learning strategies and practices which lead towards the acquisition of skills and competences seen by management as necessary for enterprise competitiveness and the effective functioning of the labour market rather than in the results or outcomes of the process. This approach, while based mainly on behaviourism and cognitive theories of learning, also draws from functionalist and contextual theories which emphasise situatedness and interaction. For the purposes of the ESRC project, we will adopt this approach in trying to explore and understand CVT innovation not in a vacuum but within the totality of the system in which it is embedded. Anyway, the very nature of CVT, that is, training carried out in the context of a work setting involving learning embedded in the work and production process, makes it necessary to examine CVT in conjunction with the specific external and organisational context within which it takes place.

As Danau and Sommerlad point out, the confusion that exists around WBL is attributable in large part to the shift in paradigmatic thinking which has not yet been fully grasped. The individualistic orientation has been so strongly grounded in VET systems as well as in learning theory and its practical applications that up until very recently there has been little recognition that the re-evaluating of what constitutes enterprise competitiveness and the re-imagining of organisational life beyond corporate boundaries, calls for new models of learning that stress the collective rather than the individual.

Clearly, this has a number of serious implications for CVT provision at company level which has traditionally been geared towards the individual and towards technical/'hard' skills. However, what today's organisation of production requires from employees are more intangible attributes, such as employee loyalty, commitment and positive orientation to continuous improvement. Such developments warrant further examination as to the extent to which CVT has changed to take into account these more difficult-to-define areas.

What is CVT?

In general, CVT is seen as relating to training undertaken within a work context after initial vocational training. In this sense, it is developmental, building upon skills or experience. Although the structure, provision and quality of initial training will inevitably influence the demand for and provision of CVT, the latter is taken to refer to any training which is carried out in the context of a work setting. As such it can be on-the-job, off-the-job, structured or unstructured.

In terms of the actual form of CVT, there is a wide range of alternatives ranging from the traditional 'sitting by Nellie' and 'learning by doing' methods to the much more sophisticated interactive computer learning packages. Table 1 presents a brief overview of various training methods and the underlying learning principles (adapted from Burgoyne, 1977; Frade, 1996, pp 38-48).

Table 1: Training and development activities and principles of learning

Type of training activity	Implicit principles of learning
Lectures and syllabus-based programmes, eg, case studies, project work	Assumes people learn by organising, sequencing and relating new information to existing bodies of knowledge
Programmed learning, eg, computer-based training, language laboratories	Based on the premise of *conditioning*: sufficient practise, feedback and reinforcement will change the habitual behaviour of learners
Behaviour modelling, eg, role play learning processes, jobrotation	Learning premise of *trait modification*: aims to skill trainees in certain predetermined learnable attributes
Business stimulations, eg, production workshop stimulations	Learning via *trial, error and feedback*: the learners operate in a designed environment where they learn to cope with relationships which result from their own interactions, rather than those built into the 'game' by the designer
Action learning and outdoor development programmes, eg, Quality Circles, regular discussion meetings of work groups, research corners, etc	Attention switched from the learners' behaviours to their '*cognition map*' of the world: through shared experience, reflection and insight are encouraged via heightened self-awareness and reinterpreting experiences in new ways; focus on participative modes of continuous learning
Experiential learning	Based on *experiential learning theory*, involving the total person (feelings, motives and emotions as well as cognition and behaviours): the principles of learning are autonomy and accommodation and the removal of barriers to allow the natural growth process

Understanding the links between the two is important in matching the appropriate training/ learning process to the learning goals one seeks to address.

The actual form of CVT and in general training provision is contingent upon the actual characteristics of the organisation.

What are core competences?

Core competences have become important for a number of inter-related reasons. These range from the changing nature of production, requiring

workers to become more flexible and adaptable to the emergence of knowledge-based jobs in the post-Fordist industrial era, demanding 'process competences' that can be transferred across different occupations. As Sommerlad notes, whereas the Taylorist paradigm was captured by the statement 'the company thinks for the worker', the new paradigm advocates a worker 'who thinks for the company', that is, a shift from being externally organised to being self-organised (Sommerlad, 1996, p 2).

There are two quite distinct types of discourse in relation to core competences. One relates to individuals with core competences typically understood as personal skills, attributes and dispositions which can be applied or brought to bear on different activities in diverse work contexts. The other focuses on the organisation and has arisen primarily in the North American organisational literature. Here the concept of core competence relates to the distinctive competences developed by a company which form the basis for its position in the marketplace. This concept of core competence derives from what Prahalad and Hamel have defined as the organisation's "strategic intent and strategic architecture" (Prahalad and Hamel, 1990).

While the notion of core competences (and its many variants, such as key qualifications, basic or generic skills, personal transferable skills) is quite popular, it is a highly ambiguous term. There are varying understandings of what core competences are, how they might be derived and operationalised, the ways in which they might be addressed in the workplace, who should take primary responsibility for their development, and where such learning should take place. The notion of core can refer to their stable and enduring character, their generic nature (common to most forms of work), the idea of transferability across jobs, occupations and even sectors, or their critical importance for realising the strategic intent of the organisation (Sommerlad, 1996, p 11).

As a result of the conceptual fuzziness which characterises the field of core competences, there are many different listings and typologies of core competences required by workers in the changing work environment. The status of these lists of competences and the way in which they have been derived is often not clear (Sommerlad, 1996, p 12). In some cases they are lists of what employers see as desirable competences in all workers; in others they derive from an analysis of technological and organisational changes and refer to the basic skills that are shared by many workers; sometimes they are grounded in task-centred skills analysis emphasising autonomy and control as an important dimension of job skills; and occasionally, core competences are identified through situational analysis which takes into account the relationship between skills, roles and the activities in which they are used.

One can distinguish four different ways of conceptualising core competences:

1 Metacompetence or metacognitive skills, ie, the intellectual skills involved in competent learning and problem solving. These are seen as fundamental in enabling workers to adjust to changes in organisational structures, technological innovation and constant change in work processes.

2 Basic competences or core skills[6], ie, the core body of knowledge and skills that must be learned as a foundation for all other learning. Typically, these skills include literacy, numeracy, personal and social skills. Information technology skills are increasingly included here. As Koike and Inoki found in examining work-centred skill formation in Japan and South East Asia, a new kind of core skill is required by workers, namely the ability to handle changes and problems associated with new integrated systems of production. They called this type of acquired knowledge 'intellectual skill' (Sommerlad, 1996, pp 16-17; see Zuboff, 1988).

3 Integrated model of competency (for the various relevant sets of competences see Sommerlad, 1996, pp 18-20): the ability to act within an occupation which is dependent on the holistic integration of technical, methodological, social and behavioural competences. This reflects a shift from defining competences in terms of a bundle of disparate skills to a more holistic contextualised approach.

4 Organisationally embedded competency (for discussion on corporate memory, see Cibbora and Schneider 1992): the outcome from the interaction between skills, technical infrastructure, roles and organisational social system. According to this approach, skills are not specific to a job or a person, but result from the interactions between system, person and job.

In general, there has been a shift in emphasis from an understanding of core qualifications as a static description of skills to a more developmental focus, in other words, on the process by which individuals move from being novice to expert and the contextualised acquisition of job and role-related competences. The last approach to core competences is the most extreme version of this trend.

What is a 'learning organisation'?

An overview of recent developments in the domain of training would be incomplete without a reference, albeit brief, to the concept of the 'learning organisation'[7]. As with core competences, there are various definitions of what constitutes a 'learning organisation'. The most frequently cited definition of the learning organisation in the European literature is that of Pedler et al: "the learning company is an organisation that facilitates the learning of *all* its members and continuously transforms itself" (1991, pp 1, 25; for a US perspective see Senge, 1990).

An important feature of the learning organisation is its emphasis upon all members of the organisation (Mabey and Salaman, 1995, p 323). It is insufficient to be focused on selected groups, at whatever level of the organisation. The notion is that individuals learn together in a collective 'system', where the learning of one individual or group is likely to have knock-on effects on the learning of another. Where the organisation attempts to restrict this transfer of learning, it is unlikely to be acting in the spirit of the learning organisation. This has clear implications for organisations which follow a strategy of polarisation of labour in terms of training and development opportunities.

Despite its appeal, the concept of the learning organisation is not devoid of problems, both in its conceptualisation and its empirical application. As with the concept of human resource management (HRM), it has a unitary frame of reference, that is, that everyone in an organisation wants to learn and help others learn. The assumption behind the 'learning organisation' is that individuals are willing and ready to participate more fully in decision making and self-directed learning. Reflection requires personal change that might not be desired by the individual or might not be feasible in many organisational contexts (Danau, 1996, p 5).

In addition, as more organisations decentralise, establishing strategic business units with responsibility for cost and profit levels, the short-term perspective of those units pulls in the opposite direction to the longer-term, developmental orientation of HRM. In such a case, short-term financial criteria operate against longer-term strategic HRM developments, such as investment in training. This is further underpinned by management reward systems which are still geared towards 'hard' financial, and often short-term, goals (especially in the UK). At a more general level, this is just another example of the contradictions inherent in the much advocated HRM model. Other contradictions that can affect the effectiveness of CVT include the simultaneous advocacy of individualism and teamwork; commitment to a job and flexibility (particularly numerical); development of a strong culture and need for adaptability.

Management resistance to change (Keep, 1989, pp 123-4) is another barrier to the wider adoption of the principles of the learning organisation. It is open to question how willing management is to work with a better-educated, better-trained, more self-reliant and, most importantly, questioning workforce. The poor education and training of managers themselves, especially in the UK, combined with a series of limiting assumptions on their part about the levels of knowledge and skills required and used by their employees are likely to stand in the way of a recognition of the importance of investing in people. As a number of studies has shown, management, especially line management which is increasingly involved in training, is the weak link in the implementation of training and development policies (Rainbird, 1994, p 340). In fact, "managers in the UK have often tended to regard a lack of training on the part of their workforce as something that does not constitute a serious problem" (Keep, 1989, p 119). In general, current models of learning organisations are highly aspirational, normative and prescriptive. They have not been empirically tested but have been used as inspirational devices to influence greater use of learning at work.

In fact, it can argued that the learning organisation debate has brought a number of issues to the fore. Contrary to organisational learning, which has tended to concentrate on formalised and prescriptive development and training needs, generic sets of competences and the adoption of universalistic assessment, the learning organisation switches attention to the process of learning, the individuality of learning styles and creating the right environment for experiential learning to occur. In addition, the debate has prompted the realisation that learning is as much acquired through emotion, attitudes, communication and habit mediated through imitation of role models, the forging of meaningful relationships, experience and memory, and developing a sense of self and values. Its focus on informal learning processes (contrary to the formal focus of many human resource development strategies) highlights the fact that a considerable amount of learning in the workplace takes place in an informal way (self-directed learning) or incidentally (Danau, 1996, p 6).

On a final note, the central conundrum of the learning organisation is: if management can be learned, can learning be managed? How can we relax control over the learning process while at the same time channelling the benefits from it? (Jones and Hendry, 1994, p 160).

Innovation in CVT and transfer

Another important area in the debate of CVT is innovation and its potential for transfer. These themes are briefly discussed in this section.

What constitutes CVT innovation?

Innovation is a complex and multifaceted construct, whose meaning is contested by researchers within different paradigms. Using an operational definition of innovation we can see innovation as 'the adoption and implementation by the enterprise of new forms of training which are considered by the enterprise as novel'. In this context, innovation refers not only to the actual content or object of innovation, for example, new training materials and/or methodologies, but also in the process by which new learning and training arrangements are introduced into or developed at the workplace.

Previous work at the Tavistock Institute has already identified a number of CVT- or WBL-related innovations (for case examples see Tavistock Institute/European Centre for Work and Society,

1996). This work highlighted innovations in a number of domains:

- *pedagogical:* learning islands; using the Leittext method[8] in structuring 'learning by doing'; structuring learning experiences at the workplace; learning models in car manufacturing in terms of embedding learning in the production process; and introducing employee development schemes;

- *organisational:* changes in work organisation; decentralisation of learning; changing roles of training officers; learning related to continuous improvement and business development;

- *institutional:* WBL experiments for the unemployed.

Another area in which there have been significant innovations is the provision of wider opportunities through open and distance learning activities which are not immediately job-related[9].

The above brief discussion is mainly concerned with innovation in the content and delivery of CVT. However, if we adopt a much wider definition of CVT innovation, we should look at the whole process and the main actors that take part. In such a case, we should look at the target groups involved, at the recipients of CVT innovation, some of whom might be quite new, and at the organisational implications that CVT innovation might have for companies and sectors. In this case, we should examine the way CVT innovation has been introduced and implemented in an organisation, barriers to transfer and new organisational arrangements that have emerged as a result. At a more general level, we should explore innovative arrangements in terms of cooperation on training issues within the context of partnerships and networks between sections of organisations, companies, sectors, and so on.

What are the main issues related to transfer?[10]

Again, previous work at the Tavistock Institute has highlighted the main issues concerning transfer and transferability. (Within the context of the project the notion of transfer can apply to the transfer of training and learning across nations, regions, sectors and organisations.)

Transfer as process

One of the main findings has been the need to see transfer as a process involving 'inputs', a 'process' and an outcome. As a result the emphasis should be placed on the way in which transfer occurs. Seeing transfer as a process where direct replication is seldom possible makes the issues of adaptation or tailoring and implementation critical factors for success.

Considering transfer as a process in which an organisation is involved means that organisational components and processes will interact with transfer. Consequently, the context within which transfer occurs becomes quite important as the actual combination of these elements will differ between organisations, sectors, regions and nations. In understanding transfer, one needs to understand the context within which the 'model' or training solution has emerged; the context, needs and capacity of the receiving environment; and the actual process of adoption including adaptation and embedding.

As learning does not take place in a cultural and social vacuum, what one learns and how it is learned can by no means be separated out of the participation in the social practices. Transfer of learning arrangements from one context – be it organisational, sectoral, or national – to another cannot be separated from the social practices of the contexts involved. It is thus difficult to see the transfer of learning as a mechanical 'move' of some tangible things – whether learning packages or training arrangements – from one context, organisation or country, to another. In this respect two basic principles derived from learning theory become quite important in understanding transfer and transferability:

• relationships between the training to be transferred and social institutions, legal frameworks, labour markets, etc, are more important than the content of transfer;

• understanding of these relationships is crucial for a successful transfer.

It is worth noting that, apart from the outer context (which is briefly discussed in the next section), culture[11], both organisational and national, is an important factor that can either facilitate or impede the process of transfer. Although there is disagreement as to which of these cultures is more important, with Hofstede insisting that national culture is more important than organisational culture and Moss Kanter arguing the opposite (Danau, 1995, p 2), there is little doubt that culture and the various sub-cultures influence international, inter-sectoral, inter-organisational, and even intra-organisational cooperation and transfer. Again this has a number of implications for the transfer potential of CVT innovations among companies, sectors and nations, with research highlighting the importance of cultural fit or symmetry between the actors involved in transfer.

Objects of transfer

In terms of the transfer process itself, this can involve both multiple objects of transfer and multiple models and mechanisms of transfer. Objects of transfer can refer to either knowledge-based and/or 'materials'-based transfer, with the former being quite intangible (for example, know-how, expertise) and the latter being tangible and concrete (for example, training materials, training-related computer software). In the middle of the continuum one finds training methodologies and infrastructures.

Depending on the nature of the transfer object, there are varying degrees of difficulty in the transfer process. For example, transfer of knowledge and know-how, or transfer of products between similar settings, requires little or no adaptation. In contrast, transfer of training products and/or methods between dissimilar settings requires a sophisticated adaptation process. In general, the higher the level of contextualisation of the transfer object (for example, training methodologies, firm-specific training, management of training resources), the more difficult the transferability. Alternatively, the lower the level of contextualisation (for example, generic training materials, principles of training or delivery systems), the easier the process of transfer.

Models of transfer

There are three models of transfer, ranging from replication to adaptation (Turbin, 1995, pp 9-12), each of which has different implications for transfer. Specifically, the transfer of knowledge tends to be associated with a type of transfer akin to learning or 'awareness raising'. The main outcomes of this process are usually exchange of knowledge and experience, and an increased understanding of, and exposure to, other settings. This type of transfer is the probable outcome of exchanges, placements, networks and dissemination events, and in general is seen as having fewer transfer barriers since the object of transfer is intangible and as such decontextualised.

The inspiration or adaptation model is another type of transfer which incorporates some degree of adaptation. Here the emphasis lies on the process by which products and/or training solutions which have been developed in one setting can be adapted and used in another. This model includes both needs analysis of the 'recipient' and 'decontextualisation' of the transfer object, as well as context-specific tailoring, and is particularly well suited where the symmetry between host and receiving settings is low, for example, CVT provision in large organisations rather than in small and medium-sized companies.

Finally, the third model — the replication or export model — is relevant when the object of transfer is generic and/or there is a high degree of symmetry between settings coupled with the appropriate infrastructure and delivery arrangements.

Clearly, the model of transfer is dependent on the object of transfer and how 'tangible' (and therefore contextualised) it is, as well as on the degree of fit between settings or the perceived barriers to transfer. Transfer of knowledge and know-how or of products between similar settings requires no adaptation, while transfer of training products or methods between dissimilar settings requires a sophisticated adaptation process. In some settings it is also possible to opt for a partial replication of

training-related products, where the transfer process involves the export of appropriate elements.

Among the mechanisms of transfer, that have been identified within the context of European programmes for example, are:

- *mobility programmes:* placements and exchanges aimed at raising awareness;

- *networks:* partnerships between education and industry, consortia of companies in particular sectors, groups of SMEs combining for the purposes of training development and delivery;

- *joint action measures:* pilot projects to develop training materials.

Clearly, in different contexts we would expect different mechanisms of transfer as each mechanism has different implications for transfer.

Barriers to transfer

Research has identified a plethora of factors that can impede the transfer process. These may be operational to a greater or lesser degree depending on the object of transfer, the process of adaptation and the potential outcomes intended. It is not possible to speak of transfer barriers as if they apply equally regardless[12]. In general, transfer barriers can be either 'internally' situated (ie, manifest in a particular partnership, exchange, placement or network arrangement) and/or externally situated general and/or systemic (ie, usually outside the immediate environment of transfer, for example, lack of transparency of qualifications or occupational skills).

In summary, the main barriers to transfer are: differences in the orientation of national policy and/or company strategy; incompatibility of culture between host and receiving country; differences in the availability of resources and funding; differences in the organisation and regulation of education and training; lack of transparency in occupational skills, qualifications and accreditation; lack of infrastructure to facilitate transfer, for example, lack of access to appropriate networks; non-inclusion of national authorities or other legitimating bodies resulting in non-legitimacy or authority; attitudes to VET in different settings and between different groups; differences in the values put upon training and qualifications by groups within or between societies; differences and rigidity in institutional arrangements; funding mechanisms and maturity of VET system; differences in industrial sectors and organisation of firms; stage of industrial development.

Factors facilitating transfer

The above list of factors hindering transfer does not mean that training-related transfer is impossible to implement, especially with regard to highly contextualised objects, for example, the way training is delivered in a particular setting. Rather it serves as a reminder of the issues that one should take into account when dealing with transfer and transferability of training. In addition, research has highlighted conditions and factors that can 'facilitate' transfer. These include organisational, structural and strategic symmetry (ie, strategic and cultural fit between partners); involvement of actors at strategic levels who could facilitate transfer and/or act as in a brokerage role; ensuring relevance to users, for example, through a needs analysis. In particular, symmetry or compatibility between different contexts is an important factor in transferability, as in some cases there is a need to ensure commonality or similarity between settings (or partners/actors), for example, where products are tangible and highly contextualised.

In general, areas where commonality can enhance transferability are:

- basic principles upon which education or training provision and delivery are based, for example, a system based on a commitment to underpinning theoretical knowledge and practical experience would contrast with one where work-based learning and output driven assessment was the norm;

- funding of education and training, particularly the statutory obligations of employers towards the training of employees and the role and importance attached to CVT;

- the role and involvement of social partners in agreements (national, sectoral and company based) over training;

- the stage of development of industrial sectors and organisations and their main characteristics in terms of size, technology, ownership, markets, competition, and so on.

Finally, transferability needs to take into account the transfer object and its contextualisation, symmetry in transfer settings, the types/definitions of transfer and the transfer process. There is a positive relationship between transferability and homogeneity, longevity, similarity in goals and complementarity in market position.

'Outer context' or situational factors

We would strongly argue for a contingency approach to CVT, as CVT provision and innovation depends on the nature of the environment in which the organisation operates. As a result, apart from the internal organisation-specific factors that can have an impact on CVT, the external environment plays a significant part in the process.

How skills are defined and provided for is highly influenced by the national structures of educational provision, methods of work organisation and the style and institutional arrangements of industrial relations (Maurice et al, 1980). The work organisation in enterprises in a particular country tends to legitimise and reinforce the way the educational system is structured[13]. As a result, one cannot understand the organisation of work and related training provision within enterprises without simultaneously understanding the development and operation of a national VET system and the interdependencies between them.

The extent to which a national VET system is 'voluntarist' (a system which has little or no government interference and leaves training to the choice of the individual or the organisation as in the UK), or 'directed' (a system where the existence of state legislation or regulation has an element of compulsion for employers to train their staff as in France and Germany), has clear implications for the way training is organised at company level. For example, the 'voluntarist' tradition in the UK has been considered responsible for the relatively low level of training provided by employers.

Related to this is the orientation of government strategy with regard to high skills/high value added versus low skills/low price economy and the respective role of state intervention or lack of it. In addition, there may be regional and/or sectoral policies on skill formation which also have an impact on CVT provision at company level.

Legal and institutional arrangements set the parameters within which companies must operate and also have bearing on training provision at company level. The existence of funding mechanisms regarding training (for example, training levy, subsidies, tax relief), contractual agreements over training, equal opportunity policy as regards training, legislation affecting levels of pay, working conditions and health and safety, all have an impact on training activity.

Labour market structures are also crucial in understanding employers' recruitment and training practices. At a macro level this refers to supply factors such as the basic level of (un)employment and skills shortages as well as demand factors such as recruitment policies or factors which determine what type of labour is needed by employers. Within the context of this project the relationship between the process of skill acquisition and labour market structure is of particular importance. For example, occupational labour markets, with their focus on a standardised mix of skills that can be transferred between employers, have different implications for skill formation than internal labour markets. The latter involves a process of skill formation which relies on training for highly specific, and therefore less transferable, skills. In this model of skill development the role of employers in providing CVT is definitely enhanced.

Last, national culture is another important contextual factor affecting CVT provision. National culture, as embedded within the different institutions of society, is reflected (and shaping) in societal attitudes to learning/training; establishes the value placed on education and training by employers, unions and the general population; and

also affects training-related strategies at company level.

Each of these factors combines to shape the assumptions and priorities of those responsible for training in a given organisation. An interesting challenge for researchers is to identify how these interrelated factors affect the decision-making process of a company in relation to CVT provision and innovation.

Conclusions

Contrary to old, static views of vocational training, which tended to regard training in a fairly deterministic way, our knowledge and experience increasingly point to the fact that vocational training is anything but a neutral and mechanistic response of companies to objective market pressures and technological changes. Indeed, vocational training (and related innovation) can be seen as a terrain of multiple interacting phenomena. In this chapter we have tried to highlight a number of issues to be taken into account when attempting to study any schemata of skill formation and related training. In our view, work-based learning and continuing vocational training are closely linked to issues of transfer and innovation: indeed, these are themes that, along with the concept of the 'internalisation of the situated enterprise', we will pursue in our fieldwork.

Notes

[1] Although the terms WBL and CVT are not interchangeable, as WBL tends to have a wider scope than CVT, a number of conceptual issues, such as those described in this chapter, show a high degree of commonality between the two. For the purposes of this study, WBL is relevant to CVT in highlighting the workplace as part of an organised learning process and in providing a learning environment that supports informal and social learning.

[2] However, one should not assume that this new model of organisation widely discussed in the

management literature is the predominant one in companies. Laur-Ernst distinguishes between three possible organisational models: (i) computerised neo-Taylorism; (ii) polarised production labour; and (iii) qualified, cooperative production labour. The first model he suggests is still predominant in many companies, whereas the third model is only realised in a very limited way. The most realistic option for the near future seems to be the polarisation and internal differentiation of jobs (see Sommerlad, 1996, pp 3-4).

[3] Again there is a long-standing debate regarding the extent to which new technology and modes of production have resulted in the upskilling or deskilling of labour (see Ashton and Felstead, 1995, p 242).

[4] However, one should bear in mind that there is a wide range of alternative competitive strategies, for example, cost minimisation, growth via take-overs. Significantly, the leading examples of human resource management (and training) are companies producing single or closely related products, rather than conglomerates or holding companies (see Keep, 1989, pp 120-1).

[5] Evidence shows that there is an increasing range of training and learning opportunities for a narrowing core workforce and a relative lack of opportunities for the majority of the peripheral workforce (see Forrester, 1996).

[6] In many countries it is assumed that these types of skills will be developed in the school system and are thus not the concern of the enterprise. Their particular emphasis in the UK reflects the until recently high proportion of early school leavers and what has been described as the nation's 'low skills economy'.

[7] It should be noted that the 'learning organisation' is different from the concept of organisational learning. In the latter learning is framed by the specific goals and objectives of the organisation. All training and development activities are linked to the pursuit and achievement of these goals.

[8] The Leittext method was originally developed in the 1970s at the Daimler-Benz training centre in Gaggenau. It aims at developing professional, technical and key skills of low skilled workers in a very structured way with a explicate focus on an independent and active role of the learner. In the Leittext method the trainer stimulates learning at all stages without setting boundaries to the actions taken by the learner. Professional competencies focus on the ability to plan, execute and monitor one's work independently.

[9] One of the most interesting innovations in this area is Ford's Employee Development and Assistance Programme (EDAP), launched in 1989. This allows for employees to qualify for personal development activities. EDAP offers every Ford employee a wide range of courses and other opportunities for personal and career enhancement, ranging from Open University degree funding to assistance with health-related programmes. The scheme is separate from the company's traditional job-related training provision which is ongoing. While Ford's EDAP scheme is best known and has been described as the 'trailblazer', there is a rapidly growing list of companies involved in similar projects, for example, Jaguar, Rover, Midland Bank, British Telecom, Kodak Ltd.

[10] This section of the chapter is based on work on the transferability of training and learning carried out in an earlier phase of the project. It also incorporates other relevant work done by the Tavistock Institute including the *Research action on transfer and transferability of training and learning* (1995).

[11] Cultural factors worth considering in the transfer of education and training are the existence or not of literacy (a graphic versus a literature culture); the social structure (in other words, differential distribution of material and cultural resources); and the pedagogic relation (relationship between teacher–learners, interaction patterns and teaching and learning styles, and pacing of training and criteria for its evaluation (see Frade, 1995).

[12] For example, where the intention of transfer is to raise awareness by giving individuals an opportunity to spend time in a foreign working environment, the barriers to such transfer may be relatively minor. In contrast, the development of a training programme, methodology or training materials intended for wider transfer may meet with barriers

which result from different accreditation and qualifications systems, differences in the arrangements for CVT or initial training between organisations, sectors, regions and nations, and differences in the values put upon training and qualifications by different groups within or between societies.

[13] Related to this is the level, quality/adequacy and location of initial education and training. Models of schooling – school/college based versus enterprise initial training – schooling/dual/mixed models of education and training (see Furth, 1985) – employer-led versus education-led/college-based models (see Green, 1991) – enterprise-based/institutional/dual models (see Calloids, 1994).

References

Ashton, D. and Felstead, A. (1995) 'Training and development', in J. Storey (ed) *Human resource management: A critical text*, London: Routledge, p 242.

Burgoyne, J. (1977) 'Management learning developments', *BACIE Journal*, vol 31, no 9.

Calloids, F. (1994) 'Converging trends amidst diversity in vocational training', *International Labour Review*, vol 133, no 2.

Cassels, J. (1990) *Britain's real skill shortage and what to do about it*, London: Policy Studies Institute.

Cibbora, C. and Schneider, L. (1992) 'Transforming the routines and contexts of management, work and technology', in P. Adler (ed) *Technology and the future of work*, Oxford: Oxford University Press.

Danau, D. (1995) *Organisations and transferability*, European Centre for Work and Society.

Danau, D. (1996) 'Learning as a strategic tool for organisations', in D. Danau and E. Sommerlad (eds) *Work based learning: Findings, policy issues and an agenda for future actions*, Tavistock Institute/European Centre for Work and Society.

Danau, D. and Sommerlad, E. (eds) (1996) *Work based learning: Findings, policy issues and an agenda for future actions*, Tavistock Institute/European Centre for Work and Society.

Forrester, K. (1996) 'Lifetime education and the workplace: A critical analysis', Paper presented at the Conference on Training and Development, University of Warwick, 7 May.

Frade, C. (1995) 'An overview of learning theory in relation to the cultural factors affecting learning and its transfer', in Tavistock Insitute, *Research action on transfer and transferability of training and learning*, Tavistock Institute.

Frade, C. (1996) 'Models and theories of learning', in D. Danau and E. Sommerlad (eds) *Work based learning: Findings, policy issues and an ageda for future actions*, Tavistock Institute/European Centre for Work and Society.

Furth, D. (1985) *Education and training after basic schooling*, Paris: Organisation for Economic Co-operation and Development.

Green, F. (1991) 'The reform of post-16 education and training and the lessons from Europe', *Journal of Education Policy*, vol 6, no 3, pp 327-39.

Jones, A.M. and Hendry, C. (1994) 'The learning organisation: adult learning and organisational transformation', *British Journal of Management*, vol 5, p 160.

Keep, E. (1989) 'Corporate training strategies', in J. Storey (ed) *New perspectives on human resource management*, London: Routledge.

Mabey, C. and Salaman, G. (1995) *Strategic human resource management*, Oxford: Blackwell.

Maurice, M., Sorge, A. and Warner, M. (1980) 'Societal differences in organising manufacturing units: a comparison of France, West Germany and Great Britain', *Organisation Studies*, vol 1.

Murray, R. (1991) 'Fordism and post-Fordism', in G. Esland (ed) *Education, training and employment, vol 1: Educated labour – The changing basis of industrial demand*, Wokingham: Addison-Wesley/Open University.

Pedler, M., Burgoyne, J. and Boydell, T. (1991) *The learning company*, London: McGraw Hill.

Prahalad, C. and Hamel, G. (1990) 'The core competence of the corporation', *Harvard Business Review*, May-June, pp 79-91.

Rainbird, H. (1994) 'Continuing training', in K. Sisson (ed) *Personnel management: A comprehensive guide to theory and practice in Britain*, Oxford: Blackwell.

Senge, P. (1990) *The fifth discipline: The art and practice of the learning organisation*, London: Century Business/Doubleday.

Sommerlad, E. (1996) 'Core competences', in D. Danau and E. Sommerlad (eds) *Work based learning: findings, policy issues and an agenda for future actions*, Tavistock Institute/European Centre for Work and Society.

Tavistock Institute (1995) *Research action on transfer and transferability of training and learning*.

Tavistock Institute/European Centre for Work and Society (1996) *Work based learning*, Tavistock Institute/European Centre for Work and Society.

Turbin, J. (1995) 'Summary of consultation exercise', in Tavistock Institute, *Research action on transfer and transferability of training and learning*, Tavistock Institute.

Zuboff, S. (1988) *In the age of the smart machine*, New York: Basic Books.

Learning from other people at work

Michael Eraut, Jane Alderton, Gerald Cole and Peter Senker

Introduction

This chapter presents findings from one aspect of the Sussex University project on the development of knowledge and skills in employment (Eraut et al, 1998). This involved double interviews, 6-12 months apart, with 120 people operating at a professional, management, team leader or technician level in 12 organisations. These were medium to large organisations in the engineering, business and healthcare sectors. The approach adopted was to find out what types of work activity our respondents were currently conducting, what types of knowledge and skill were entailed, how they had acquired the capability to do what they now did, and what factors had affected this learning process.

Learning from other people and the challenge of the work itself proved to be the most important dimensions of learning for the people we interviewed. Although some reported significant learning from formal education and training, this was by no means universal and often only of secondary importance. This confirmed our view that the dominant assumption that learning in *The Learning Society* comes only from recognised formal provision needs to be balanced by more empirical evidence about what, how, where and why people learn at work. There was also a need to understand more about factors affecting this informal and mainly self-directed learning and how it was situated within working contexts and personal life histories. Without such evidence the current wave of visionary literature about learning organisations is in danger of remaining at the rhetorical level. We sought to provide some guidance on important policy questions, such as:

- Is it possible to enhance the quantity and quality of informal learning at work?

- If so, how might efforts along these lines be most appropriately conceived?

- What then would be the role of more formal education and training?

- How would this affect the role of managers?

- What would be the implications for approaches to staff development at the organisation level?

The research literature on informal learning at work is very thin and somewhat overshadowed by practitioner literature advocating that it be given more attention and advising people on how to promote it. This is usually illustrated with success stories about organisations which have established reputations for their innovative approaches, but backed by very little evidence from independent evaluations. Three studies stand out. Gear et al (1995) interviewed 150 professionals about a recent 'learning project'. Following Tough (1971) they defined a learning project as,

the equivalent of at least one working day over the last three years spent developing some aspect of your professional knowledge, skills and competence to the point where you could pass some of it on to a colleague. (Gear et al, 1995, p 8)

Our evidence covered this semi-planned type of professional learning, but also a wide range of learning that did not meet this particular definition. Nevertheless their evidence both for

informal learning and for significant learning from other people (reported by 92% of their respondents) was very strong. However, they do not provide much detail about the contextual factors which gave rise to this learning. The image presented is that of an independent professional rather than that of a professional worker in a large organisation, perhaps reflecting their very different sample. This 'independent professional' ethos can also be found in a long-running programme of excellent studies by researchers into continuing medical education in North America (Davis and Fox, 1994; Fox et al, 1989). This research is deeply situated in the physicians' work environment and professional lives; but again the sample is very different from our own. Finally Mumford et al (undated) have recently reported research into the learning of 144 board members/directors of 41 organisations, concluding that in most organisations formal management development programmes had been relatively ineffective. Informal learning on the job was of greater importance, but learning opportunities at work were not sufficiently used.

To address the implications of our project for the policy questions listed above, this chapter will need to be read in conjunction with its successor, *The impact of the manager on learning in the workplace* (Eraut et al, 1999). This present chapter is divided into three main sections: organised learning support; consultation and collaboration within the working group; and learning from people outside the working group.

Organised learning support

We interpret the term 'organised learning support' as referring to any form of support for people's learning which requires special organisation. The main kinds of activities reported (not necessarily in our terminology) were: apprenticeship; induction; mentoring; coaching; rotations; visits; shadowing; and reference to experts. Though never subversive these activities were not necessarily organised in any official way, and knowledge of them was often confined to the immediate work unit. It was also possible to discern different assumptions about learning underpinning the selection and transaction

of modes of learning support. Thus the practices we noted resulted from the interaction between:

- the prevailing level of formality and structure in the workplace;

- the initiator(s): the learner; the organisation; the line manager; or another (usually more experienced) colleague;

- the assumptions about learning held (but not often overtly stated) by the parties involved.

Assumptions about learning

Five main approaches to the facilitation of learning could be distinguished, which operated sometimes on their own and sometimes in combination.

Induction and integration

This focused primarily on people becoming effective members of their work unit and the organisation as a whole. The emphasis is on socialisation: understanding the purposes and goals of the unit and the organisation, their own roles and others' expectations of them; and fitting into the interpersonal nexus in which their work is embedded. The management approach can vary from laissez faire and light monitoring to a succession of formal events, for example, an induction course followed by other short courses. The latter will normally be part of a whole organisation approach, which local managers may or may not follow up. It is associated not only with new employees but also with planned changes in the organisation's policy or culture.

Exposure and osmosis

These are frequently used to describe the process of learning by peripheral participation. Through observations and listening the exposed learner picks up information and know-how by a process of osmosis. The role of the manager is limited to that of enabling sufficient exposure to a diversity of contexts and situations, but otherwise remains passive. However, the learner has not only to be alert and receptive but also to work out what they need to know. Shadowing and certain types of rotation and visit are the usual methods employed.

Self-directed learning

This approach assumes that the learner takes a more active role, learning from doing the work and finding out on their own initiative what they need to know. Such an active role is more likely to be adopted if the work is appropriately chosen and the learner encouraged in their learning. As with the first two approaches, managers' hopes that employees will be self-directed learners may not be realised if their attitude is perceived as permissive rather than positively supportive.

Structured personal support for learning

This involves the use of supervisors, mentors or coaches. Sometimes this is an official process; sometimes the role is assumed by a manager or a more experienced colleague; sometimes a manager asks someone to provide help and advice; sometimes the learner is encouraged to seek advice from a particular colleague or group of colleagues. Whether officially organised or not, the climate of the workplace is likely to affect significantly the quality of learning support.

Performance management

This approach is being introduced by an increasing number of organisations. It involves regular appraisal and target-setting, but its emphasis can vary from a 'stick and carrot' approach to motivation, to a developmental approach focused on learning to improve personal performance. These competing attitudes towards performance enhancement have been debated by managers and management theorists for at least 50 years. At its best, performance management facilitates learning through discussion about and provision of learning support. At its worst, the learning entailed in improving one's performance is not recognised and hence discouraged.

We shall now consider some examples of organised learning support and comment on them in the light of the above analysis.

Mentoring and coaching

Example 1

Some middle managers approached our respondent about the idea of mentoring. They discussed it, talked it through and found out more. The respondent sounded out some senior colleagues who agreed to be mentors and now they have "regular monthly one-to-ones". No formal time is allocated and it is not part of a senior manager's job role. Our respondent only involves people who are able and willing to be mentors, those who want to contribute something and are prepared to give up the time.

"If you say to every senior manager 'You must be a mentor for someone', they do it probably badly and probably grudgingly. And that's not of much benefit to the individual." (Senior manager insurance company)

Example 2

"Basically, they just give you some new death claims and they'll sit with you and show you what to do for the first few, then you start doing it yourself. Then they go away and you have to do it, and you pass it on to them to check it, and after a while you're just left to do it all by yourself ... they sample your work once a month and from that they can identify any problem areas which you might have. They look to correct those." (Insurance claims technician)

Example 3

*"I've been on an interviewing skills course, which was quite early on ... in terms of developing my skills in that area I feel I was coached quite effectively ... I sat in on a number of interviews to start with, then I was interviewing along with somebody else ... and after that I was able to gain feedback from them as to how I had got on ... then I just got on with it on my own, which I much prefer ... as long as I have got the skills...."
(Graduate trainee – personnel)*

Example 4

A radiographer wanted to expand her range by doing mammography. It was agreed she would do a course to get the certificate. This involved some formal teaching, visits to other departments (surgical, path lab, radiotherapy) to find out about their involvement in diseases of the breast. In addition she works for part of the week alongside a woman who already has the certificate and a lot of experience. This woman goes out of her way to show her relevant things that come up when she's not there, shows her lab reports on mammograms she has done, etc, thus building up her expertise more quickly.

Comment

Mentoring is focused on problems and situations of concern to the mentee, as well as with their general progress. In Example 1, the reason for an informal, voluntary approach was explained in terms of commitment and quality, but the support itself was delivered in quite a structured way. In Example 4, training was provided by a course which had a built-in requirement for visits, but the coaching aspect was offered voluntarily by a senior colleague. The manager supported the course and arranged a rotation involving both the exposure/osmosis and the self-directed learning approaches, but the volunteer coach converted this into structured personal support for learning.

Example 2 describes a standard coaching system designed for a particular purpose, adaptive to individual rates of progress and incorporating phased withdrawal of support and follow-up monitoring. Example 3 is another case where a course provides some structure and the coaching is fairly informal but still carefully phased. We also encountered many examples where courses of this kind were not accompanied by any planned follow-up in the workplace, so learners had to work it out for themselves and were generally less clear about issues of quality.

Rotations, visits and shadowing

Example 1

"I've been doing this job for ... 18 months now, and essentially all the skills that go with this technical coordinator job, I learnt from my predecessor, and so I've taken over from somebody, and, that wasn't sort of a few weeks' handover. For a good six months or more, we were working alongside each other, and as I picked things up.... He'd been doing it for about two years previously ... I'd had contact, I'd taken over from him when he went on leave before, but that was very much, just keep it ... you know, caretaking." (Engineer)

Example 2

A senior cardiac technician in a district hospital has negotiated a day a week working in a teaching hospital. His reasons are "keeping in touch with other technicians", working on "more technically challenging cases" which "keep your skills up" and taking videos of local cases to get other opinions about them.

Example 3

"I went to Korea in '85. I'd been in for half a year troubleshooting, and the managing director and I noticed that they had some very good systems for how they dealt with product introduction. They, they went through a [type] of pilot phase before they started in serial production – just to make sure that the serial production would not be hit by any faults on the main product, because it would put them, the whole business, in jeopardy, and again I learnt a skill there, a way of working." (Engineer)

Comment

Examples 1 and 2 show an unusually high investment in learning. Both come from organisations where there are high risks associated with mistakes. The first concerned an important technical services role in a large organisation where technical stoppages incurred very high costs and loss of reputation. The second concerned quality of care for high risk patients. Both were officially organised, though in the second case the rotation was initiated and negotiated by the technician himself. Both assumed a mixture of learning by exposure and self-directed learning.

Example 3 is better described as a special assignment than a rotation or a visit. The significance is that what was learned had nothing to do with the purpose of the assignment which was more to do with giving than receiving information.

Designated experts

This was a strong feature of a large telecommunications company with a substantial research and development commitment. Several respondents referred to certain people as 'technical experts' or 'technical heroes', but this designation had no official status.

> *"Luckily the guy that actually helped me to get the job turned out to be one of the main experts in the department.... He's just one of these people that knows everything about everything that you need to know ... he's a technical expert.... And the brilliant thing is, he talks ... I think he's a natural teacher anyway ... I'm battling over something and he'll go up to the whiteboard and draw two circles and a line and it'll all fall into place." (Software engineer)*

Learning who the experts were and how to use them was part of the integration or socialisation process, and reasonably reliable in this particular company. In other companies, however, this could be a lengthy process often involving a chain of personal contacts.

Conclusion

The examples presented in this section have been positive. Negative examples where the absence of these kinds of organised support for learning on-the-job left people struggling were too numerous to count. Learning was often much slower than it needed to be. Without further analysis, we cannot judge whether these examples are representative even of positive examples, but we are fairly confident about one distinct difference between our evidence and the prevailing

perspective of the human resource development literature. Very few of our positive examples resulted from organisation-wide strategies or initiatives. Most were relatively informal and initiated by middle managers, colleagues or the learners themselves. Where there were positive examples of organisational initiatives they were more likely to be in the financial sector than in healthcare or engineering.

Consultation and collaboration within the working group

Groups and teams

Almost all the people we interviewed identified themselves as members (and sometimes also the manager) of a group of people, but the nature of this group and of the interactions between its members varied considerably. This is reflected in the vocabulary used to describe it. A term like 'department' or 'unit' indicates merely that a group of people occupy a common space on an organisational chart and share a common manager. It does not necessarily mean that they work in the same place or that they are the exclusive occupants of their normal work-space. Overt use of the term 'group' usually implies either collocation or a shared function with regular liaison meetings, as well as introducing an affective dimension to the discussion which indicates its significance for a person's work identity. This affective dimension is even stronger when the word 'team' is used and accepted by all members of the group, but its rhetorical use by managers is resented when the designation of a group as a 'team' is not shared. The word 'team' implies a significant degree of collaboration and interdependence, where outcomes should be judged at group rather than individual level.

When studying the impact on learning, the most important variable is the style of normal interaction in the workplace. Since departments or units can be large and dispersed or small and intimate, co-membership is not on its own a useful indicator of an actual or potential working relationship. Hence we have defined the term 'working group' to indicate a group of people who have regular contact with each other at work, some sense of shared purpose, and no stronger allegiance elsewhere in the organisation. Learning from people with whom one does not have such regular contact, even though they may happen to be in the same unit or department, is discussed later.

We also found it useful to distinguish between normal groups with a common manager and special groups to which people may be allocated for a fixed period on a part-time or full-time basis: these groups are more likely to have a leader, coordinator or chairperson than a manager. In normal groups we discerned three main types of learning situation: ongoing mutual learning and support; collaborative teamwork; and observing others in action when one is only a peripheral participant. Special groups, intra- or cross-departmental, are usually charged with a specific task – for example, review, audit, preparation of a decision or policy brief, problem solving – and engage in large numbers of meetings with varying amounts of independent or collaborative work in-between. We also found that people learned from special assignments in which they represented their working group in an external context.

The distinction between collaborative teamwork and ongoing mutual consultation is often unclear. The most obvious examples of collaborative team work entail group tasks on which people work together, contributing different skills. If they have separate parts of the task to work on individually, the extent to which their individual work is discussed in the group and the relative amount of time spent individually and in groups will be critical factors. One obvious example would be a hospital operating theatre where interdependence is crucial. The members of a theatre 'team' have to learn to work together but their level of mutual consultation varies widely. We encountered several small teams of engineers with complementary skills working together on a succession of problems, and cross-professional teams such as cardiologist and cardiac technician, radiographer and consultant. People reported how such work helped them to recognise knowledge and skills which they did not themselves possess and how their knowledge of tasks and situations was broadened by their continuing contact with people who had different perspectives. The process of learning to work with other people

was often mentioned as transferring to other, less intensive kinds of group situation.

Several situations were reported which raised the question of when a group becomes a team. Two factors in particular seemed to affect this: the advent of a crisis and the strength of the affective dimension. Groups of individuals working in parallel with occasional consultation could become transformed into teams when confronted with a major problem or deadline; sometimes this had a lasting effect as people began to recognise each other's contributions and group identity was strengthened.

> *"The team I am in is absolutely fantastic. They've worked brilliantly, everybody does everything, including Q who's my manager... It's like when it's contract round it's everybody get round busy, they work hard and they play hard – it's as simple as that. And as I say, everybody mucks in. It's just a good working environment, you enjoy coming to work, you know that if you've worked 11 hours one day you're not expected in at 8.30am the following day." (Contract manager, energy supply company)*

Gradual development of interpersonal support which extends beyond the workplace also contributed greatly to team feeling among certain working groups. This is more likely to happen when the work is emotionally demanding, as, for example, with a group of nurses on a ward.

> *"It's getting involved with the people that you're actually learning with and supporting each other, I think that's what comes through isn't it. It's where you support each other, if you see that somebody's struggling with something and you found it particularly easy or you worked it out, then you can help each other. The same thing happens when you're struggling, you can say to someone how the hell did you do that. It's give and take isn't it. That's how we tend to work on the ward as well, we support each other, you know. It doesn't have to be a nursing problem, it can be anything, it doesn't matter what it is.... We all tend to help each other, it's very good team work on this ward, actually." (Hospital nurse)*

Many wards lack this collaborative ethos; yet it does not take much deliberation to recognise that strong affective bonding among staff is likely to have a significant effect upon the quality of care.

Ongoing consultation and observation

When people spoke about collaborative teamwork, mutual learning tended to be assumed as an integral aspect of it. With other types of working group, there was more overt discussion about learning from each other. Indeed, when we began our fieldwork we were surprised by the amount of learning which occurred through mutual consultation and support. For many people this was the most important mode of learning. Often learning was triggered, almost forced upon people, by the challenge of the work itself, but even this learning was frequently facilitated by consultation with others.

"You just learn as you go along, and people are quite happy if you ask, as I have done on several occasions.... Q said if I get one of those, he'll quite happily come and give me a hand, 'cause obviously I wouldn't be expected to know how to do that straightaway." (Newly qualified radiographer)

Typically such consultations would entail a request for quick advice, seeking another perspective on a problem, help with a technical procedure or information on whom to ask for help on a particular issue. The way in which learning from colleagues happens can be very different in a new activity from how it happens in an established one. In a start-up activity, knowledge and skills are being acquired in a multitude of ways and can flow from person to person in several directions at once. In contrast, one person may acquire a large measure of the skills and knowledge needed directly from a predecessor in an established activity, perhaps by means of mentoring.

Another mode of learning – observing others in action – was frequently cited in relation to interpersonal skills (although many of the examples cited were negative rather than positive).

"I've seen customers with members of staff where they've almost locked horns across the desk because the customer and the member of staff are both, kind of stubborn, neither of them will want to back down ... you'll never get anywhere if you're like that. And I think by watching other people you learn things yourself and pick up ... you would see a situation and you would know that that's not a situation that you want to get yourself into." (Personal banker)

"So you can learn by other people's mistakes and I think that's where I have actually picked up a lot of things because I think, God, I wouldn't talk to somebody like that or, I wouldn't like to be spoken to like that, and I think to myself, I wouldn't dream of asking anybody to do something on the ward that I wouldn't do myself." (Ward sister)

The role of special groups and assignments

An engineer reported learning a lot from membership of a review group.

"We have a trouble reporting system, which I had to learn how to use, and then we implemented things and got processes working from there. And I just sat in on the meetings, where ... the other expert designers corrected and reviewed test cases and other documentation for corrections, and I just used that as a good background to bounce loads of questions off." (Software engineer)

She then went on to describe how she had identified a member of the group as a useful learning resource.

"Others view him as arrogant, but he's not that at all. He goes out of his way to help people and he views his job as there to help us, because he knows so much, and he also wants to help, like, new designers and testers, because he feels that he can learn so much from them as well.... In the review, he's the kind of person that'll question, 'Why have you done this? Who is your audience?' The things that I'm saying that people don't do, he demands when he's in a meeting ... [but] he's very approachable." (Software engineer)

In contrast, a radiographer reported somewhat sceptically a move to formalise a review process which was already happening on an informal level.

"She has sort of set up a monitoring programme, where every now and again we're supposed to look at the films we've done and be honest with ourselves and assess how good they are: whether they're perfect; whether they're good; or whether they're adequate. Once you've done that you're supposed to just, you know, ask another radiographer's opinion, to see if you agree, and then discuss about it ... I think the fact that she's got the

certificate gives her the enthusiasm, she sort of sees it as her area." (Radiographer)

A ward sister described how becoming a member of the hospital ethics committee gave her many valuable cross-professional perspectives. However, a more important outcome was her development of a patient advocacy role and the confidence to speak out for patients, not only in official meetings, but to senior people round the hospital when appropriate opportunities arose.

> "When it comes to things like advocacy, and speaking for people who can't speak for themselves, then, I think I take that quite seriously, and people can get away with a lot, but, there's a fine line ... and if I think something is wrong I'll say it, and whether it's to a consultant or to a very junior doctor, it wouldn't bother me, because if I had confidence in myself and knew what I was doing was right, and that whatever was going on was wrong, then I would say it. I think some of that is just becoming more assertive as you become more confident in your role and in your job ... and just as a person.... It must be very intimidating for a patient when you've got the consultant in the bay and the house officer, and the med student, and the registrar, and everybody standing around the bed. They're telling you all these things they're going to do to you, and you're sitting there going, 'Yes, doctor, OK that's fine'. But then ... it is part of my role, to say, 'Well actually, no, I don't think that's fair ... you haven't given them a choice. You've told them, but when you left they said to me, you know, that they don't want to do this, or they're not happy with it'." (Ward sister)

Another nurse described how her manager set up a management team to discuss issues with her senior nurses, including herself. This gave her another perspective on the work of the ward, and also enabled her to understand what was involved in working as a manager. So she was far better prepared when she became a manager herself.

An engineer commented that once a problem was publicly acknowledged and a group set up to tackle it, people who had previously kept quiet started sharing their knowledge. It was highlighting the need which triggered this different response.

Feedback within the group

Feedback from colleagues is a prominent feature of the diagnostic radiographers' environment because they are accustomed to looking at each other's pictures and commenting on them. This was done in a very relaxed way, so that comments were not taken personally, and it facilitated a great deal of group learning. They also put red dots on pictures to indicate to casualty officers where they had noticed that something was broken, thus contributing to diagnoses by often relatively inexperienced doctors without trespassing on their traditional territory.

A community nurse described several ways in which feedback from her manager had both given confidence and led to learning. For example, after she had done a special project on handling and preventing falls, he asked her to prepare some posters on it, to present them to students, then later to make them available to other nurses and doctors. He gave positive feedback on the performance of delegated task, and, if not entirely happy, gently asked if other possibilities could have been considered.

> "A couple of times he's actually said, 'Well, you know you could have done so and so', and I said, 'Oh, I never thought of that', and he says, 'Well you'll know next time', or, 'We'll talk about it' or whatever.... He's not actually disagreed with me, he's said 'Have you thought of doing so and so?'. He doesn't say, 'You shouldn't have done that', he doesn't say it like that. He'll say 'Well perhaps you could have done such and such', and I think, 'I could have done that'." (Community nurse)

An insurance company manager described how when he first came to the company he got most help from immediate peer colleagues, particularly in understanding the company culture, but now he was learning more from his subordinates than his colleagues. In a vivid example he explained how he had been to two management assessment centres in connection with a job, then:

> "I got the feedback, and the first thing I did was photocopy it and take it round my team and said 'There you go, that's my feedback, how are you going to help me with this?', or, 'How can you help me with this?', or, 'Do you agree with it?'.... You're actually getting some

feedback from them, sort of validating the data really. We do it in a semi-light hearted way, I mean they sort of say, 'Did you really say that in this team exercise', or whatever, and we have a chat about it." (Insurance company manager)

Another manager relied on a particular colleague for honest feedback:

"One of my colleagues, Tina, is very helpful because she provides me with feedback that other people don't. So in fact she is very honest with me ... basically she says I think you may have upset such and such ... or maybe I could have done this ... I can actually learn from that and build any bridges if I need to ... so she's very helpful." (Regional manager, bank)

Learning from people outside the working group

People outside the immediate working group can be usefully divided into three categories: those in what one might call an extended working group, with whom there is regular contact; people in one's own organisation with whom contact has to be specially arranged, sometimes through a common acquaintance; and people outside the organisation altogether. Examples of the first category – the extended working group – included a fortnightly meeting of personal bankers from different branches, a cross-departmental committee and healthcare professionals seeing the same patients. In this last case learning from doctors often occurred by peripheral participation in ward rounds or clinic.

People within the organisation

Various reasons were cited for seeking help from people in parallel positions in one's organisation. For the newly arrived or newly promoted it was often practical help with common organisational procedures such as tendering or preparing specifications. In one case there was also strong affective support:

"In the first few weeks of starting the F grade, Liz, our G grade, was away and our ward clerk was also away. When the two of them are away it was basically ... you

know ... it was me. I think that was a bit scary but it was quite nice because I thought well if I can cope for these couple of weeks on my own, then I'll cope.... You're learning as you go along, and if you know there's things that you've never done before then there's lots of people that you call on. Other F grades, other G grades in the hospital, will phone, and did phone and say, 'Is everything all right?'." (Hospital nurse)

For others it was keeping abreast of the micropolitics of the organisation, getting early information about changes of people or policies, getting advice about when, to whom and in what way to put forward a proposal. This nearly always took place in an informal setting, over lunch or in a bar, using networks created by people who used to work together or met on an in-house training course. These meetings were also used to get feedback about the work of one's own unit.

"Maybe somebody's havin' a real gripe about the way you put a new system in, and the fact that none of the users get trained adequately or something, and they're much more likely to say that off the record, over a beer or something, and have a real gripe about it." (Manager, engineering company)

In several cases critical information for one's work had to be sought elsewhere in the organisation and this often required some initiative. For example, learning where the services are located in a large and complex building is notoriously difficult. One service engineer we interviewed was constantly debriefing people about what went where. He made considerable effort to be present wherever new services were being installed, which he might later have to modify or repair. We also interviewed an installer who emphasised the need to talk to the people who designed the telecommunications equipment he was about to install. Sometimes people realised with considerable concern that an individual elsewhere in the organisation had unique knowledge which they needed:

"We've had a callout from [a company] about performance measurements ... I've gotta get to another guy who knows about [it], and he's got to go in and look at it for me, and I'm saying to him, 'Look, you really have to sit down one day' ... it's only one guy who knows about this application, and we've gotta sit down with him, and he's gotta show us. The only other way is to do what he

did. He just tinkered around, and he's getting knowledge through tinkering around, and we could do that, but it takes too long ... I don't have time to do that, and none of the other guys have time to do that either. So basically the quickest way of learning is to get him for a day, and say, 'Look, just take us through the basics of this, otherwise we're gonna be weeks learning this'." (Customer service engineer)*

Yet another engineering example concerned cross-departmental cooperation between a designer and a manufacturer.

"I would be good at identifying the problem, the root cause of the problem – the root cause is we don't have ... I don't know ... enough force at this point or something like that or this bit cracks because it's not expanding, so I would identify the problem and then Mike and I would sit down and we'd bounce ideas and I'd say 'Well, look, you could do this by doing that', and he'd say, 'Well, you know, it's a little bit complicated, can't we do it this way?', or, 'That wouldn't work because of this'." (Development engineer)

One company set up a special communication channel to encourage the flow of information between departments, but informal contact was still the preferred method and usually proved to be faster and more effective.

"I got to know ... people in test plant support quite well, which is quite handy if you've got a problem and you phone them up.... They have a number you phone if you've got a problem, and then they will phone one of the test plant support people, and then they will come out and see you.... They try to say, do it all officially but if you happen to bump into them and you just want to ask a quick question, they might give you a quick answer ... or they might say, 'Well phone it in, I'll come and see you in a minute'." (Development engineer)

Another informant described how he got the benefit of a course in a faster and more relevant way without having to attend it. His method was to contact the in-house expert involved, get the course materials, read for an hour or two then question the expert for a couple of hours on points of particular relevance to his work.

"Sometimes I pick up more important information because I ask the specific questions and find out the exact things, you know, go down the things which are of interest to me rather than having to [sift through general material].... A lot of it can seem rather obvious and straightforward and the bit that I'm particularly interested in isn't covered maybe in sufficient detail." (Telecommunications engineer)

Professional networks

In the healthcare sector, the working group was also extended by a rich variety of professional networks. But these networks were still largely dependent on personal contacts – A had previously worked or trained with B – often renewed by finding themselves on a course together or working for a common organisation.

"Di that works here, we trained together, and I've known her now for seven or eight years, and it's a bit like having a house sister I suppose. We're very close, but I think it's only natural that when you've been through training together and you've been through a lot of different situations that you do have that bond ... I couldn't imagine not having friends who weren't nurses or doctors. Because you can ring them up and say if you've had a bad day, and they know what you mean ... they know exactly how you feel, and they'll know exactly what to say ... and that's quite important.... Sometimes, when you have incidents that you'd really rather forget about, and you don't want to talk about it, but you know that it'll just sit inside and fester away, if it was something that happened and you think you made the wrong decision, or whatever, then [to] people like Di and Liz, I can say, 'Look, I can't sleep, this is worrying me', or whatever, and they'll know, because they've had – not the same situation – but they'll have had a similar incident where they were really worried and couldn't sleep about it, and it's quite nice just to talk it out with people." (Hospital nurse)

This nurse went on to note the absence of such support among junior doctors.

"I think sometimes with the doctors, it seems quite different. I think they seem to have a lot less support than we do, and I feel quite sorry for them really, because they seem constantly to be in situations where they've just never had to do it before, or they have no idea what they're doing." (Hospital nurse)

Our experience from other research suggests considerable variation in such support across organisations as well as between professions.

There was also some evidence of 'invisible colleges' in the health professions which extended beyond close personal contacts but also depended on occasional meetings for their sustenance.

"We've been on conferences, we do chat to the radiologist and cardiologists, and they have an input. Our radiologist is eager to develop new ideas, so we then look into it and ... assess whether it's worth pursuing. We might go to Brighton or Hastings if they're doing some new technique, to see if it would be beneficial for us to start, see what sort of results they're getting. But within South East Thames we might [ring up] another centre." (Senior cardiac technician)

"We've got people, people who are on courses at the moment, like the nuclear medicine course, we've had one last year and we've got one this year, and they come back with new ideas, and they need to do this experiment or do that experiment, see this or see that, they go off to other centres, come back and tell us all about it." (Senior radiographer)

A related example from the insurance sector was an informal mentoring relationship with a former boss.

"My old boss from 1995, he's moved on to become a director in the corporate pensions business, up in Kingswood, and I've kept in touch with him and used him as a sounding board on things like, 'I'm going to try this, what do you think?', because he's got a lot of experience in the area. 'What do you think of this, what do you think of that?' And personal decisions, 'What should I do about this job?'.... We get on well together and on the same sort of wavelength and I know he will be honest, so he just won't deal in platitudes and say, 'There you go, yes you're doing very well'." (Team leader, insurance company)

Learning from suppliers and customers

The search for knowledge by some engineers is best described as entrepreneurial. We have already described a service engineer who went to great lengths to be present whenever something new was being installed, and another who 'short-circuited' a lengthy course. Others sought to extract information from suppliers and/or customers, not just market information but also technical information. One sought to get the customer perspective on technical aspects of the equipment he installed. Another described how he had begun to acquire a more customer-oriented view of production and criticised his colleagues for giving this insufficient attention in their development of new products. A third found debriefing customers and suppliers a better way of keeping up to date than reading the journals. The following excerpt from an interview vividly describes how an energetic, problem-solving engineer makes use of several different personal sources of help.

"A lot of that information I learnt from my predecessor ... what is unique to this area, how the automation works, how it thinks, and how it progresses along its list of tasks. Because we were still developing this software, the software had bugs, so you need to have a fairly good understanding of what it's trying to do, in what sequence the software's trying to do things ... I talked in depth with the two people who actually write software and provide the hardware ... the way things work. I would be called upon when we had a problem, I would look into the problem, I may be able to solve it, or I may need to go back to ... my predecessor, and ask for advice, and he may come and help, or he may say, 'Oh yes, I think you need...'. But it is very much thrown in at the deep end, hands on.... When something unusual crops up, you have to go in at the basic level and work through the system.... If it's something provided by an outside company I quite often ring up and ask for advice ... regularly make use of outside companies who supplied equipment, always found that very useful, technical departments, much more than I have done previously in my career to be honest." (Process engineer)

Conclusions

At a theoretical level, our research strongly supports the importance of informal learning, but it also shows how strongly it is situated in the work itself and its social and organisational context. We elicited evidence of tacit knowledge in the areas of personal relations, problem orientation, and expertise in using (or repairing) particular machines or software systems, as well as knowledge that was explicitly articulated. However, a major reason for the prevalence of learning from other people was that this knowledge was held by individuals rather than embedded in social activities. While some knowledge was firmly embedded in organisational activities, other knowledge *was* located only with a small number of individuals – often only one. Thus we can consider both a continuum from tacit knowledge to knowledge in the form of written propositions, and a continuum from knowledge which is individually situated, to knowledge which is organisationally situated. Any theory of a learning organisation has to take this variety into account.

At the level of practical policy, we suggest that informal learning may be enhanced by two complementary approaches. Individuals can be helped to become more capable learners, who can be both more reflective and more self-directed, more proactive and more able to recognise and use emergent learning opportunities. Managers can be helped to take more responsibility for the quality and quantity of learning in the units which they manage. Our research suggests that a manager's indirect impact on learning through the allocation of work, as a role model and by creating/sustaining a microculture which supports learning from peers, subordinates and outsiders, is no less important than their direct impact through advice and encouragement, appraisal and feedback.

References

Davis, D.A. and Fox, R.D. (eds) (1994) *The physician as learner*, Chicago, IL: American Medical Association.

Eraut, M., Alderton, J., Cole, G. and Senker, P. (1998) *Development of knowledge and skills in employment*, Research Report No 5, Brighton: University of Sussex Institute of Education.

Eraut, M., Alderton, J., Cole, G. and Senker, P. (1999) 'The impact of the manager on learning in the workplace', in F. Coffield (ed) *The implications of research on The Learning Society for policy*, Bristol: The Policy Press

Fox, R.D., Mazmanian, P.E. and Putnam, R.W. (eds) (1989) *Changing and learning in the lives of physicians*, New York, NY: Praeger.

Gear, J., McIntosh, A. and Squires, G. (1995) *Informal learning in the professions*, Hull: School of Education, University of Hull.

Mumford, A., Robinson, G. and Stradling, D. (undated) *Developing directors: The learning process*, Buckingham: University of Buckingham International Management Centre.

Tough, A.M. (1971) *The adult's learning projects*, Toronto: Ontario Institute for Studies in Education.

The Learning Society: the highest stage of human capitalism?

Stephen Baron, Kirsten Stalker, Heather Wilkinson and Sheila Riddell

Introduction

In 1995, at the first coordinating meeting of the Economic and Social Research Council's (ESRC) Research Programme *The Learning Society: Knowledge and skills for employment*[1] following current conventions, an industrialist was invited to comment on the 13 recently successful proposals. In this case the industrialist was Peter Wickens, sometime Personnel Director of Nissan UK and author of *The road to Nissan: Flexibility, quality and teamwork* (1987) and *The ascendant organisation* (1995). Having reviewed several of the research projects in terms of ideas of vocational training, skill, employment and national competitiveness, Professor Wickens turned to our proposal, *The meaning of the learning society for adults with learning difficulties*. He expressed the view that he could not understand why this project had been funded as part of *The Learning Society* Research Programme. His reasoning appeared to be that people with learning difficulties have little or no role to play in the Gestalt of training–skill– employment–national competitiveness. It would seem that on 'the road to Nissan' some are bound to fall by the wayside. While the rush of academics and ESRC administrators at the end of the meeting seeking to distance themselves from such comments was reassuring, Professor Wickens articulates a moral, political and, perhaps, intellectual position which must be addressed.

A fully critical history of people with learning difficulties, how they have been constituted, contained and treated, remains to be written but glimpses of 19th and 20th century history are sobering (Atkinson et al, 1997; Ryan and Thomas, 1987; Scheerenberger, 1983; Tomlinson, 1982). In the Victorian era, when progress was thought to offer a solution to most problems, people with learning difficulties were gathered into asylums for education and improvement, and then returned to the community and useful work. In the latter part of the 19th century, amid a moral panic about rising numbers, people with learning difficulties as a category became medicalised as 'aments' (without minds) and this enabled the more widespread and long-term incarceration of the group. The standard medical text, *Tredgold's mental deficiency (amentia)*, was able to show, in successive editions from 1908, smiling photographs of patients next to detailed descriptions of the *post mortem* dissection of their brains (Tredgold, 1908). Occasionally individuals, such as the Genius of Earlswood Asylum, would be sponsored as *idiots savants* with some exaggerated ability being held in contrast with their general retardation (Howe, 1991). This emphasis on non-ideal bodies reached its zenith under the Nazi regime in Germany where, from 1933 onwards, the machinery for the 'final solution' was gradually assembled and people with learning difficulties became its first victim population (Burleigh, 1994; Lifton, 1986). Eugenicist thought was not restricted to the Nazi Right with such pillars of the British Left as Wells, the Webbs or Shaw advocating state-sanctioned selective breeding. Scandinavian countries, while proclaiming the rights of people with learning difficulties, continued forced sterilisation into the 1970s to maintain the purity of Nordic race (*Guardian: The Week*, 30 August 1997, pp 1-2). Similarly there have been reports that Quaker Oats funded experiments in the US during the 1940s and 1950s, which involved feeding children with learning difficulties radioactive milk with their breakfast cereal to test the effect on their digestive systems (*The Times*, 28 December 1993, p 7). Currently, in Britain, unborn babies with learning difficulties or with physical impairments are the only *category* of persons who may be aborted because of their characteristics. We may see these examples, centred around strong conceptions of fitness-for-purpose, as limited cases of what we may call the utilitarian discourse (Fevre, 1996).

Since the 1970s, constructions of learning difficulties have witnessed a decline in, but certainly not the disappearance of, medical dominance, together with the development of a social work discourse of 'normalisation' or 'ordinary life principles' directly critical of medicalisation and the utilitarian discourse (Brown and Smith, 1992). The normalisation discourse seeks variously to establish the rights of people with learning difficulties to a 'normal' or 'ordinary' life and/or to constitute them in socially valued roles by reproducing the environmental and social contexts of 'normality' as settings for warrantably 'normal' performances. One very influential formulation of such a perspective is that of O'Brien who defines five major accomplishments for services for those with learning difficulties: being present in the community; supporting choice; developing competencies; affording respect; and ensuring participation (O'Brien, 1987). Given the emphasis in normalisation on valuing all humanity, we may see these examples as limited cases of what we may call the humanist discourse.

In its formulation of a definition of a learning society the ESRC Programme appears to combine elements of both the **utilitarian** and the *humanist* discourses:

> *A learning society would be one in which* all citizens *acquire a high quality* general education, *appropriate* **vocational training** *and a* **job (or series of jobs)** worthy of a human being, *while continuing to* participate *in education and* **training** *throughout their lives. A learning society would combine excellence with* equity *and would equip* all its citizens *with the* **knowledge, understandings and skills to ensure national economic prosperity** *and much more* besides. *The attraction of the term 'the learning society' lies in the implicit promise not only of* **economic development** *but* the regeneration of our whole public sphere. *Citizens of a learning society would, by*

> *means of their* continuing education *and* **training**, *be able to engage in* critical dialogue and action to improve the quality of life of the whole community *and to ensure* social integration *as well as* **economic success**. *To define the learning society in this way is to make clear the scale of the task facing the UK.* (ESRC, 1994)

Surveying the 13 projects initially funded and the debates of the Programme meetings to date, we suggest that utilitarian elements have become dominant. Is *The Learning Society: <u>Knowledge and skills for employment</u>* (emphasis added) to be simply a new version of utilitarian discourse, (re)constituting people for the epochal changes in the capitalist mode of production (Lash and Urry, 1987), or can it combine a new utilitarian discourse with an humanist discourse more successfully than its predecessor – the social democratic combination of justice and efficiency (which died at Ruskin College, Oxford in October 1976 when James Callaghan launched 'The Great Debate' about education)? In this chapter we seek to begin to explore the possibility of this combination through an analysis of the position of adults with learning difficulties in a learning society.

In our research proposal we suggested that such adults represent a strategically important group for understanding a learning society and made a reference to Durkheim's *Rules of sociological method* (Durkheim, 1982). In his discussion of how to distinguish the normal from the pathological, Durkheim argues that a society of saints would have to invent sin: every society must have its excluded group whose very exclusion serves to define the boundaries of what can be included as normal. In a learning society those with learning *difficulties* are one, if not *the*, group whose position and experience can help us reflect on the nature of such a learning society. Does (to paraphrase Durkheim) a learning society have to (re)invent idiocy (the Victorian term current in Durkheim's day) in order to define itself?

One immediate temptation, both for audience and for authors, when faced with the tension between utilitarian and humanist discourse, is to 'split' the field into 'goodies' and 'baddies': in our case we made our proposal from within the broad assumptions of the humanist discourse. From this position a variety of critiques of the utilitarian discourse lie readily to hand. While celebrating the overwhelming importance of the world of work (the competition of skills 'out there') the utilitarian discourse is, it would appear, excluding significant parts of the population from birth (Baron et al, 1998). Such structural exclusion from employment may of course be cushioned by a welfare state (presumably, the lay-bys on the road to Nissan) which constitutes the person with learning difficulties in a separate and subsidiary discourse as the client or the cared-for. Being an adjunct to, and a cost on, the dominant discourse, the welfare discourse marginalises people with learning difficulties, reproduces their dependence and is perpetually vulnerable to being reduced to being 'nugatory'. This exclusion and dependency is unacceptable to the assumptions of inclusion and self-development central to the humanist discourse.

More fundamentally, different writers in the humanist tradition argue that the utilitarian discourse has what Wolfensberger calls 'strong death-making tendencies', the acceptance of acts of omission or commission which end the lives of devalued others (Wolfensberger, 1994). While it is easy to distance ourselves from the activities of the Nazis or Quaker Oats noted above (as being performed by a different sort of person, in a different place, in a different time), Christie, on the basis of research with ordinary Norwegians who killed in Nazi concentration camps, suggests:

> *... it is no longer to me a question of 'Why did some people kill?'; it is more a question of 'Why did some people not kill?'. (Christie, 1992, p 160)*

For Christie one "big Idea, namely the primary distinction between what is useful and what is not useful" sets no limits on what can be done to other people.

> *What would happen if there were a new crisis, perhaps a war on home territory with food shortages, with shortages of medical equipment, who would be the first to the wall in such a situation? (Christie, 1992, p 161)*

In part this question is answered by Wolfensberger (1994, p 30) who suggests that this is precisely what happened in war-torn countries in the 1980s and documents how, in the event of a nuclear accident, the contingency plans of the US provide for the

simple abandonment of people in residential care homes.

What Christie's work warns us about is the power of the utilitarian discourse to lead us to do what once seemed inconceivable; our current civilisation being a thin veneer which could be readily stripped away by hardship. Wolfensberger (1994) argues that, in fact, such practices have already arrived in Western countries. The culture of modernism makes people with learning difficulties particularly vulnerable to a variety of 'death-making' practices before birth, in infancy and in all stages of life thereafter. In their perceived weakness, impairment and vulnerability, people with learning difficulties represent, for Wolfensberger, the vanguard of a larger category of devalued people increasingly subject to death-making tendencies. He documents 13 categories of such devalued people and the practices to which they are subject.

Such critiques are trenchant: significant minorities are being systematically excluded and kept dependent; whole categories of persons, classically people with Down's syndrome, are being subjected to prenatal genetic screening and selection. Who is *allowed* to be a member of *The Learning Society* is an issue which cannot be taken for granted. Too often, however, these critiques of the utilitarian discourse are used simply to label (and thus dismiss) any dissent from the orthodoxies of the humanistic discourse. For example, in Wolfensberger's system for assessing the quality of services the strongest indicator of quality is the acceptance by managers and staff of the tenets of Wolfensberger's theory (Wolfensberger and Thomas, 1983). Not without reason has the normalisation movement been accused of having a cult-like organisation (Lindley and Wainwright, 1992). The humanist discourse as realised in normalisation also has its own humanist critics: it tends to emphasise conformity to 'socially valued roles' as a desirable goal for people with learning difficulties (often, in practice, this necessitates taking on and celebrating the perspective of the very people who devalue those with learning difficulties); it tends to discourage people with learning difficulties from associating with each other and it can thus weaken collective experience as a basis for collective action on common problems.

To limit oneself to *either* the utilitarian *or* the humanist discourse, simple or with adjuncts, is not adequate. In order to begin to define this complexity, and to reflect on the nature of *The Learning Society* by analysing the position of those with learning difficulties, we will first discuss the person with learning difficulties as worker, then the applicability of the social model of disability with its discourse of rights and dignity to *The Learning Society*, and finally the nature of supported employment and social capital.

The person with learning difficulties as worker[2]

The prominence of 'knowledge and skills for employment' is not new: since at least the advent of the factory system, the importance of education for creating an appropriately skilled and differentiated labour force has been a constant theme, if not anxiety. In what Lash and Urry (1987) call the epoch of organised capitalism (the 1870s to 1970s) people with learning difficulties tended to relate to the labour market in one (or more) of four ideal typical ways (Weber, 1949).

First the asylums – intended as a temporary, educative intervention for people with learning difficulties – became the long-term institutions with which we are decreasingly familiar. Within the confines of the asylum programmes of work (or its proxy), which may or may not have been market (sales) oriented but which were not part of the labour market in any real sense of the word, were an important part of the regime of containment and partial self-sufficiency. For example, South Ockenden Hospital, Essex, had an Industrial Therapy Unit for many years in which patients packed biros or incontinence pads for commercial contracts. Many hospitals such as the Royal Scottish National Hospital (RSNH), Stirlingshire, or Calderstones, Lancashire, have extensive farming and horticultural production for internal consumption, staffed by patients. This we term 'containment work'.

Second, for those not confined to the asylum there was what we term 'enclave work', work which is more labour-market oriented but is not open market employment. In this ideal type, people with

learning difficulties were recruited in numbers to specific locations for specific tasks, often with some form of residential provision. Commercial farms staffed largely by 'boys' from long-stay hospitals around the fringes of industrial cities were an example of this. The former Scottish neurosurgical hospital at Killearn ran a substantial part of its domestic operation with women from Lennox Castle Hospital, Lennoxtown, for whom there was a special residential unit at Killearn. The current sheltered workshops would also fall into this category.

Third, the epoch of organised capitalism supported open labour-market employment of many people with learning difficulties in particular roles. Of Glasgow special school leavers in the 1940s, the 80% who went into employment tended to find employment in 'support' of labour intensive production and distribution. The 40,000 people employed in heavy manufacturing at the Parkhead Forge in Glasgow included substantial numbers of tea-boys, canteen staff, messengers, etc (Riddell et al, 1997).

Fourth, in the age before 'community care', people with learning difficulties simply might not appear on the labour market, living within the domestic sphere, usually of their family. The particular career of a person with learning difficulties might, of course, combine elements of all four ideal types: a child placed in Lennox Castle at a relatively young age may have moved to work at Killearn Hospital with its residential provision as a young adult and, on retiring or the onset of chronic ill health, might be cared for at Killearn or return to Lennox Castle. The particular journey of a person along these routes depended critically on their 'grading' within a utilitarian system of high, medium and low grades – public identities which formed life chances.

Since the 1970s the position of people with learning difficulties in the labour market has, we suggest, undergone structural change in terms of each of these four ideal types. First there has been a major decarceration from the long-stay hospitals. The RSNH, for example, had a peak inpatient population of 1,326 in the 1970s (RSNH Mental Handicap Services, 1991, p 2) which has been successively reduced to projected 'irreducible' core inpatient populations of 624 by 1990 and 447 by

1995 (Planning and Development Team: Mental Handicap, 1988), 369 by 1997 (Pollachi, 1993, pp 1-2) and, in the current five-year plan, 30-70 'assessment' beds (Stalker and Hunter, forthcoming).

Central to such resettlement programmes, and to the lives of people living with their family of origin (our fourth ideal type), has been the issue of meaningful day-time activities for people placed 'in the community'. Community care policy changes have resulted in some people with learning difficulties wanting to, and being encouraged to, enter the labour market often for the first time. The process of decarceration has coincided with a decline in enclave work, our second ideal type. In part this has been the result of a shift in policy thinking away from the segregation implied by sheltered workshops and other such 'category'-based sites. This and a decline in employment of the third ideal type, has been affected by changes in the labour market which have both restructured or removed many of the jobs previously taken by people with learning difficulties, and which have increased the competition for those that remain. What does the changing structural position of people with learning difficulties tell us about the nature of labour in contemporary Britain, and about *The Learning Society*?

The changes in social policy noted above are part of what we have called elsewhere the 'disaggregation of care' (Baron, 1992), part of a restructuring of the welfare state. This restructuring is part of wider changes rooted in shifts in the nature of global capitalism variously analysed as 'disorganised capitalism' (Lash and Urry, 1987), 'flexible accumulation' (Harvey, 1989) or 'reflexive accumulation' (Lash and Urry, 1993), a response to which *The Learning Society* is in part. Why are people with learning difficulties the marginal group which our Phase 1 interviews with the Scottish Local Enterprise Companies (LECs) suggest that they are (Baron et al, 1998)? There is an aversion in the field to generalisation, criticised by Dumbleton (*Times Educational Supplement*, 1994) but it is crucial to see the communality of position which gives the label 'learning difficulty' a real basis.

First, as parts of the economy move towards 'economies of signs', those for whom manipulating symbols is difficult are disqualified from significant sectors of employment. While the significance of

skills in information technology can be vastly overplayed there are demands which many people with learning difficulties cannot meet. Second, 'learning difficulties' signify either a perceived slower pace of 'learning' than 'normal'; a limit to what can be learned that is lower than 'normal'; or a 'difficulty' in applying what is learned in one context to another context. In the classic 1911 text of organised capitalism Taylor's 'ox' who provided the muscle behind the different sized shovels was treated, in theory and reality, as a mechanical being for whom speed or quantum of 'learning' was of little relevance (Taylor, 1947). Similarly the classic study of Fordism (Beynon, 1973) shows the assembly line workers as adjuncts to machines with repetitive tasks requiring endurance of monotony rather than 'learning'.

Why is 'learning' suddenly so important? It would be optimistic to see the shift towards flexible accumulation as bringing with it a more fulfilling labour process: the arguments about de-skilling are powerful. What flexible accumulation does promise is perpetual instability, a permanent bourgeois revolution, where tasks change rapidly and start-up costs are to be minimised in an increasingly frantic search for profitable investment: slow learners are expensive. People with learning difficulties also tend to be slower in the performance of tasks and thus, in certain terms, less productive: slow producers are less profitable. In our interviews with the LECs these are the reasons given for the lack of success of people with learning difficulties in the competition for jobs 'out there'. Many are expected never to take up employment and either 'progress' (as required for Scottish Enterprise's outcome-based funding formula) is gradually being re-defined as a succession of training courses or, people with learning difficulties are being excluded from the LEC discourse of knowledge–skills–employment to be re-inserted into a social work discourse as clients or the cared-for.

However, there is an alternative discourse in the LECs which constructs people with learning difficulties as model employees and which suggests that prejudiced employers are acting against their own interests. People with learning difficulties are constructed as loyal, hard working and punctual. The contrast is explicitly made with other groups of workers, particularly new entrants such as school leavers and Skillseekers who are seen as lacking these virtues of obedience and conformity.

The apparently contradictory constructions of people with learning difficulties both as marginal workers and as paradigm workers are united by being part of a utilitarian discourse: the person with learning difficulties is constructed in narrow terms of how they might contribute to profitable production, such contributions being seen as deriving from the personal capacities of the would-be workers. The construction of people and their production in terms of such individual characteristics could be labelled 'human capital' and, in attempting to ally this with the new epoch of capital accumulation strategies, the query in our title, 'the highest stage?'.

The social model of disability: barriers and rights

But is this not common sense? Is it not clear that people with learning difficulties are less able and less productive than other people, in need of generous welfare support, but not part of the mainstream? In our initial interviews there was evidence of a third, minority, discourse about people with learning difficulties as workers, as people valued for their social, rather than their narrowly economic, contribution to production. In our research proposal we committed ourselves to exploring the applicability of the 'social model of disability' to those with learning difficulties and to *The Learning Society*. We highlighted the social model of disability because, in the past decade, it has been responsible for a fundamental reconceptualisation of disability away from a focus on individual impairments, medically defined, to a focus on the social relations which create barriers to full citizenship for people with an impairment (Swain et al, 1993). 'Disability' from this perspective becomes an active process of social relations, not a quality of the particular individual. The social model (and to talk of it as a unity is to ignore, for present purposes, vigorous internal debates) has been developed almost exclusively in terms of the barriers to full social participation presented to people with physical impairments – classically poor access to facilities for those with mobility difficulties.

Given the definition of *The Learning Society* quoted above, the data suggest that the utilitarian discourse is weak on participation in vocational training for people with learning difficulties. We now suggest that the utilitarian discourse is effectively silent (not only for this group) on other components of the definition of *The Learning Society*: a general education; the worth of the human being; participation in citizenship; the regeneration of the whole public sphere; equity; critical dialogue; social integration; and the whole community. What can the position of people with learning difficulties, conceived within the social model, offer *The Learning Society*?

First, applying the social model to learning difficulties moves us away from medical models of deficit towards issues of barriers; away from the neat classification of syndromes (which then stand as 'explanations') towards the question of 'why not?'. What are the barriers to people with learning difficulties participating fully in production? We have already hinted at answers: if production is organised for profit through flexible accumulation strategies, then those who are slower to adapt and slower to produce will be marginal. However, if production was organised on learning society principles of human worth, participation, social integration and critical dialogue, people with learning difficulties would be one category of producers among many.

Second, a social model conception of people with learning difficulties can help us understand skill in a more thorough way than can human capital theory. For human capital theory skill is an intrinsic quality of the individual, a real trait, innate or gained through various means, which enables certain tasks to be performed. In this conception people with learning difficulties can be seen as poor investments, the unskilled, the proletariat of *The Learning Society*. For the social model this is an active process of dispossession – a creation of incompetence through social relations rather than an intrinsic quality of individuals. If we apply this perspective to the question of skill or the question of competence, it can have powerful de-reifying effects: which groups are deemed to have special (or exclusive) possession of which skills? What does this enable them, and others, to do? Which groups are deemed not to have certain skills? What are the consequences for them and for other groups? Why are certain behaviours deemed to be 'core' skills and what are the consequences? Why are certain behaviours deemed to be 'transferable' skills and what are the consequences? For these reasons, in our proposal we committed ourselves to attempting to dismantle one such barrier by employing people with learning difficulties as researchers and we are currently supporting one such group to conduct part of the research.

If *The Learning Society* is to fulfil the humanist aspects of its self-definition, it needs to develop thinking about citizenship, participation, human dignity, social integration and the community more fully than the current utilitarian inflection of the Programme does. Analysing the position of people with learning difficulties can contribute significantly to this. In the past two decades the humanist discourse has been developed with reference to people with learning difficulties perhaps more than any other group in British society (children being the other main group). The right of people with learning difficulties to an ordinary life have been subject, as noted above, to much definition, with *Learning Society* themes of participation, human dignity, social integration and the community much to the fore. In a real sense the construction of people with learning difficulties over the past 20 years has traversed some of the terrain which *The Learning Society* is seeking to map. What are the lessons of this?

Positively the development of this discourse of rights has defined sets of human rights which, if applied to the ordinary lives of ordinary people, would be revolutionary. For example, substantial attention has been paid to ensuring that work, or its proxy, for people with learning difficulties is organised in such a way to be as fulfilling as possible. Rights to dignity and respect, and their practical realisation in different settings, have been developed. The nature and realities of choice have been explored and mechanisms of social integration defined. What 'citizenship' and 'the community' mean have been subject to much debate. The humanist repertoire which is the goal of *The Learning Society* has been well developed with people with learning difficulties and awaits further study: its implications are profound. Just as proponents of the social model of (physical)

disability argue that lowering (physical) barriers to disabled people makes life better for all people, we suggest, ensuring that the ordinary life of those with learning difficulties realises human rights might function to realise such rights more widely.

Negatively, the development of this discourse has been, at a minimum, ambiguous. The major realisation of this discourse has been through a professional struggle between social work and medicine, with the humanist discourse acting as a professional power/knowledge for social work. This has lead to the bureaucratic definition of rights, with a variety of competing manuals available. Such definitions create rights as abstract in the sense that they appear as entries in the manuals rather than as the reciprocal products of ongoing social relations. The professional power/knowledge which produces the person with learning difficulties as the bearer of rights simultaneously re-subordinates that person as the passive consumer of rights defined, and imposed, by others. However, in part the discourse has developed through the activism of organisations of people with learning difficulties, such as People First. Much can be learned from this experience of a subordinated group organising itself and articulating its own definition of 'rights'.

How can *The Learning Society* begin to articulate a new combination of the utilitarian and humanist discourses, avoiding the weaknesses of both as noted above? In order to begin to formulate an option we finally turn to an analysis of people with learning difficulties, supported employment and the circulation of social capital.

Supported employment and the circulation of social capital

In recent years supported employment *projects* run by voluntary organisations have become one of the vanguard policies for people with learning difficulties (Beyer, 1995). Originating in the US, the term is used to cover a wide variety of different schemes, core components of which are open employment; individual rather than group placement; and job coaches; but the absence of subsidy to the employer (unlike the British state-funded Supported Employment *Programme* which does subsidise employers). In a supported employment project a person with learning difficulties finds a job in the open market and, with the help of a coach, learns to perform the tasks on site, thereafter holding employment as normal (but with supplementary support available if needed). The preferred name for such projects is Real Jobs [Placename]. Such schemes combine elements of both utilitarian and humanist discourses. The motivating force behind the projects is strongly humanist (ordinary life principles), while there is a strong utilitarian inflection in terms of coaching of the person with learning difficulties in the skills of the job, forming a quantum of human capital.

The concept of 'social capital' has enjoyed a similar prominence in recent thinking about the organisation of production (Coleman, 1990; Fukuyama, 1995). These conceptions of social capital stand as a neoconservative rejoicing in the final triumph of (a certain version of) American liberal capitalism (Fukuyama, 1992). We offer a version owing more to Marx's critique of fetishism and collective labour (Baron et al, 1998). Rather than seeing social capital as a quantum, greater or smaller, with an independent reality, we suggest social capital is a process in which social relations are formed and reformed with material consequences. Viewed from this perspective the introduction of a person with learning difficulties to a workplace through a Supported Employment Project offers a strategic opportunity for both the analysis and expansion of social capital.

If social capital is to be a serious concept for analysis, rather than as another quantity to be measured alongside physical and financial capital (Coleman, 1990), we need to understand its processes of circulation and reproduction, to see as processual that which appears as given or objective (or which is invisible in its omnipresence). As suggested above, the person with learning difficulties is, by definition, something of an 'outsider' – Schutz's spontaneous stranger (Schutz, 1974) – for whom the seen but not noticed may have to be explained. The introduction of a person with learning difficulties (plus job coach) into a workplace may be seen from this perspective, not as an isolated moment of human capital formation (teaching the skills), but as a moment when the usually hidden nature of social capital is made apparent.

In terms of *The Learning Society* some of the dimensions of the contribution of people with learning difficulties to a learning society, viewed from such a social capital perspective, may be outlined in terms of the key components of the Programme's definition (see p 50 of this chapter):

- "*All citizens*" requires inclusion. The boundaries of 'in' and 'out', of 'normality' and difference, are made visible and challenged by the introduction of people with learning difficulties to 'real jobs'. This may range from challenging non-specific fear of people with learning difficulties, through the celebration of difference, to challenging the nature of very specific job demarcations and status differentials.

- "*... a high quality general education and* **appropriate vocational training**" demands greater clarity about the combination of humanist and utilitarian discourses. Where the range of possible learning is thought to be restricted, and pressure to train for specific tasks heightened, what constitutes the essence of a high quality general education? How it may be taught and assessed must be defined with more care than is perhaps usual. Appropriate vocational training is clearly central to people with learning difficulties taking up 'real jobs' and defining the nature of such training is a major task for supported employment projects. Improvements in vocational training necessitated by supported employment projects can be expected to benefit a wider population.

"... a job (or series of jobs) *worthy of a human being*" raises fundamental questions about production and how the utilitarian and humanist discourses can combine. As noted above, issues of human worth, its definition and its defence, have been extensively considered in relation to people with learning difficulties. The difference in the workplace of people with learning difficulties, and any tendency to their devaluing, confronts general questions of human worth and its relation to the current material and social organisation of production.

"*... to participate* in *education* and **training** throughout their lives" describes the life trajectory of many people with learning difficulties. Many people move from one round of training to another with little intrinsic satisfaction or extrinsic outcome in terms of employment. How personal development and preparation for the external demands of production might be combined is a question which has been often posed but seldom answered in the field of learning difficulties.

"*... excellence with equity*" prompts basic questions about the evaluation of tasks and social differentiation. The ability to perform which tasks is highly valued (or not) and what are the criteria for these evaluations? What is the social distribution of these evaluations and what are their material and social consequences? For a group whose performances are often not constructed as 'excellent', where can equity be found?

"**... knowledge, understandings and skills to ensure national economic prosperity** *and much more besides*" contains the revealing contrast between a confident specificity about the needs of national prosperity and a vagueness about the other matters to which education and training could contribute. As we have suggested above, the construction of people with learning difficulties, either as marginal workers or as paradigm workers, gives crucial insight into the reality of such required 'knowledge, understandings and skills' for a wider segment of the labour force. Insofar as people with learning difficulties are a group for whom, and sometimes by whom, ideas of what constitutes an ordinary and dignified life have been explicitly elaborated, there is at least an initial agenda for debate. This agenda has been heavily structured by professional interests and gives a warning about the process by which such definitions are developed. The imperatives of a learning society of inclusion and participation demand that people, with or without learning difficulties, are centrally involved in their own self definition.

"*... the regeneration of our whole public sphere*" and "*critical dialogue and action to improve the quality of life of the whole community*" signify issues of active citizenship. As a group sometimes deprived of current benefits of citizenship the processes of extending citizenship has been explored with people with learning difficulties. As a group whose quality of life has often been low, people with learning difficulties have (had) defined some of the dimensions of 'quality of life'. As the improvement of physical access for people with mobility difficulties has benefited wider sections of the population, we might expect improvements in the life of people with learning difficulties to benefit other groups – both in terms of substance and in terms of learning from the process of extending citizenship.

"*... social integration* as well as **economic success**" contains the key dilemma of *The Learning Society*. Can the competitive logic currently posited as essential to economic success be allied with social integration except through the unthinking conformity at the heart of Fukuyama's 'trust' (Fukuyama, 1995)? On *The road to Nissan* the very presence of people with learning difficulties poses questions about routes and destinations which some would prefer to be left unasked.

We believe Professor Wickens to be profoundly wrong.

Notes

[1] Hereafter *The Learning Society* will be used to denote the ESRC Programme, *The Learning Society* to denote the general concept.

[2] This argument has been extended in Baron et al (1998).

References

Atkinson, D. et al (1997) *Forgotten lives: Exploring the history of learning disability*, Kidderminster: British Institute of Learning Disability.

Baron, S. (1992) 'Innovation and regulation in the care of those with special needs', in S.R. Baron and J.D. Haldane (eds) *Community, normality and difference*, Aberdeen: Aberdeen University Press.

Baron, S. et al (1998) 'The best burgers: the person with learning difficulties as worker', in T. Shakespeare (ed) *The disability reader*, London: Cassell.

Beyer, S. (1995) 'Real jobs and supported employment', in T. Philpot and L. Ward (eds) *Values and visions: changing ideas in services for people with learning difficulties*, London: Butterworth Heinemann.

Beynon, H. (1973) *Working for Ford*, Harmondsworth: Penguin.

Brown, H. and Smith, H. (1992) *Normalisation: A reader for the nineties*, London: Routledge.

Burleigh, M. (1994) *Death and deliverance: Euthanasia in Germany c1900-1945*, Cambridge: Cambridge University Press.

Christie, N. (1992) 'Six ways to deal with stigma', in S.R. Baron and J.D. Haldane (eds) *Community, normality and difference*, Aberdeen: Aberdeen University Press.

Coleman, J.S. (1990) *Foundations of social theory*, London: Harvard University Press.

Times Educational Supplement (1994) 'The other end of the rainbow' [by P. Dumbleton] 19 March, p 3.

Durkheim, E. (1982) *The rules of sociological method*, Houndsmill: Macmillan.

ESRC (Economic and Social Research Council) (1994) *The Learning Society: Knowledge and skills for employment: research specification*, Swindon: ESRC.

Fevre, R. (1996) 'Some sociological alternatives to human capital theory and their implications for research on post-compulsory education and training', paper to the European Conference on Educational Research, University of Seville, 25–28 September.

Fukuyama, F. (1992) *The end of history and the last man*, New York, NY: Free Press.

Fukuyama, F. (1995) *Trust: The social virtues and the creation of prosperity*, London: Hamish Hamilton.

Harvey, D. (1989) *The condition of postmodernity*, Oxford: Blackwell.

Howe, M.J.A. (1991) *Fragments of genius: Investigating the strange feats of idiots savants*, London: Routledge.

Lash, S. and Urry, J. (1987) *The end of organised capitalism*, Cambridge: Polity Press.

Lash, S. and Urry, J. (1993) *Economies of signs and space*, London: Sage.

Lindley, P. and Wainwright, T. (1992) 'Normalisation training: conversion or commitment', in H. Brown and H. Smith (eds) *Normalisation: A reader for the nineties*, London: Routledge.

Lifton, R.J. (1986) *The Nazi doctors: Medical killing and the psychology of genocide*, New York, NY: Basic Books.

O'Brien, J. (1987) 'A guide to lifestyle planning: using the activities catalogue to integrate services and natural support systems', in B.W. Wilcox and G.T. Bellamy (eds) *The activities catalogue: An alternative curriculum for youth and adults with severe disabilities*, Baltimore, NJ: Paul Brookes.

Pollachi, D. (1993) *Proposed merger of RSNH and Community NHS Trust and Forth Valley Healthcare Directly Managed Unit*, Larbert: RSNH.

Planning and Development Team: Mental Handicap (1988) *Joint initiatives: Forth Valley/Central Region*, Stirling: Forth Valley Health Board.

Riddell, S. et al (1997) 'The concept of the learning society for adults with learning difficulties: human and social capital perspectives', *Journal of Education Policy*, vol 12, no 6, pp 473-83.

RSNH (Royal Scottish National Hospital) Mental Handicap Services (1991) *RSNH Community Trust: Application for NHS trust status*, vol 1, Larbert: RSNH.

Ryan, J. and Thomas, F. (1987) *The politics of mental handicap* (revised edition), London: Free Association Press.

Scheerenberger, R.C. (1983) *A history of mental retardation*, Baltimore, NJ: Paul Brookes.

Schutz, A. (1974) 'The stranger', in M. Natanson (ed) *The collected works of Alfred Schutz*, The Hague: Martinus Nijhoff.

Stalker, K. and Hunter, S. (forthcoming) *The relocation of people with learning difficulties from Scottish hospitals*, Stirling/Edinburgh: University of Stirling/University of Edinburgh.

Swain, J. et al (eds) (1993) *Disabling barriers: Enabling environments*, London: Sage.

Taylor, F.W. (1947) *The principles of scientific management*, New York, NY: Harper Row.

Tomlinson, S. (1982) *A sociology of special education*, London: Routledge.

Tredgold, A.F. (1908) *A textbook of mental deficiency*, London: Balliere, Tindall & Cox.

Weber, M. (1949) *The methodology of the social sciences*, Glencoe, Ill: Free Press.

Wickens, P. (1987) *The road to Nissan: Flexibility, quality and teamwork*, Houndsmill: Macmillan.

Wickens, P. (1995) *The ascendant organisation*, Houndsmill: Macmillan.

Wolfensberger, W. (1994) 'A personal interpretation of the mental retardation scene in the light of the "signs of the times"', *Mental Retardation*, vol 32, no 1, pp 19-33.

Wolfensberger, W. and Thomas, S. (1983) *PASSING: Normalisation criteria and ratings manual* (2nd edn), Toronto: National Institute on Mental Retardation.

Skill formation: redirecting the research agenda

David Ashton

Introduction

The conventional approach to the analysis of skill formation processes tends to focus on education and formal training as the main components. This is partly a consequence of the dominance of human capital theory with its emphasis on education and training as an investment for the individual, the employer and the society. The analogy with physical investment encourages the view of training as a series of finite activities, the more one invests in education and training the greater the return in terms of earnings, productivity and economic growth. The necessity to provide a convenient measure of this investment leads academics to focus on formal education and training provision, as these can be readily derived from government statistics. Years of schooling and length or frequency of training provide convenient measures of the investments made by individuals, organisations and countries in the process of skill formation. As a result the two tend to become equated[1].

This is reinforced by public discussion and individuals' perceptions. At a national level, political debate concerning the development of the nation's human resources tends to focus exclusively on education and training: the assumption being that if we can increase investment in education and training we will automatically receive benefits in the form of increased income, productivity and national wealth. At the individual level, findings from research on employees' perception of training suggest that they too tend to equate training with formal training, either on-the-job or off-the-job. Less formal modes of learning, such as informal on-the-job training and self-initiated forms of learning

at work are less likely to be perceived by individuals as training (Felstead et al, 1997). It is not surprising that training tends to be perceived by all parties as a series of one-off activities delivered through formal courses. However, this concentration on training in discrete time-bound units in formal institutions as the loci of the process of skill formation is now being challenged from a number of sources.

An academic, Michael Eraut, in this volume and elsewhere, has pointed out how a great deal of learning takes place within the workplace, independently of the provision of formal education and training, and how the discourse about lifetime learning has been dominated by the providers of formal education and training (Eraut, 1997). Meanwhile, outside academia, perhaps the most significant of these challenges comes from the changing practices of employers and changes in the structure of organisations. For example, the globalisation of capital flows and product markets; the success of companies from Japan and the Tiger economies in securing substantial parts of world markets for products ranging from ships to electronics and automobiles; the relocation of some labour intensive industries to the low-cost Asian economies. All these have intensified competition in the Western world. Companies have responded by reducing the amount of labour they employ, delayering management and producing flatter organisations. In addition, they have sought to reduce labour costs by out-sourcing aspects of the production system and some of their services and increasing the productivity of remaining staff by techniques such as teamworking, multiskilling and enhancing the commitment of employees to the goals of the organisation. In the public sector the programmes of privatisation and the deregulation of sectors such as finance and transport have produced similar pressures with similar effects on the structure of organisations. The result has been that some organisations, but by no means all, have undergone major shifts in their internal structures which, together with the incessant drive to reduce costs, has had important implications for the process of learning at work.

Organisational change and learning at work

Traditionally, large organisations, such as automobile manufacturers and banks, have organised their training through a centralised training function which delivers a series of programmes from which line managers and employees can choose to participate. The delivery of training and the analysis of the organisation's training needs remains the province of a specialised training function. There, learning takes place in the classroom or workshop under the guidance of a specialist trainer or instructor or through a computer-based training programme designed by a specialist trainer. The training programmes are designed to deliver knowledge and skills ranging from specialised technical skills to organisational procedures and new technology. The individual employee has access to them at a time determined by the central training function and then has to apply the new knowledge/skills in the workplace[2].

This approach to training is designed to deliver specific skills, to enhance the performance of employees in one particular aspect of their job in organisations where roles are clearly specified and circumscribed. Jobs are clustered in departments or functions, responsibilities are precisely specified and each individual employee occupies a position in a clearly defined hierarchy of authority. Rewards are linked to clearly specified outputs, for example, the number of widgets produced or telephone calls handled per unit of time. Training is geared to improving any particular aspect of the employee's behaviour deemed problematic, for example, to improve manual dexterity, to enhance technical knowledge of specific product process or service, but other aspects of the employee's behaviour are considered irrelevant to their performance of the job.

As organisation structure changes, moving in the direction of more flexible forms with fewer layers of authority, a greater emphasis on teamwork and multiskilling, this produces what Lawler (1994) terms a move from job-based to competency-based structures. This in turn produces change in the 'training needs' of the individual employee. As responsibility is pushed further down the line with the reduction in the number of hierarchies, and more employees take on managerial responsibilities, their roles are broadened as their responsibilities increase, and cognitive skills become more important. The introduction of teamwork demands new skills in collaboration with colleagues and group working. The broadening of the work role demands that new skills are learned.

A number of studies in different societies (Bertrand and Noyelle, 1989; Kelly, 1989; O'Reilly, 1992; Thompson et al,1995) have identified similar new skills emerging around three main themes. The first is problem solving: the ability to comprehend the whole process of production, including both technical knowledge and knowledge of the organisation, and to make decisions within that broad framework. The second is teamworking: the ability to work collaboratively in pursuit of a common objective, to share information and communicate effectively, often referred to as social skills. The third is elementary management competencies: the ability to operate in changing conditions; plan time; prioritise; and operate strategically in relation to organisational objectives[3]. These are not skills or competencies that can be readily acquired from one-off courses.

One further consequence of recent organisational changes is that the leaders of an organisation become more concerned with shaping the overall values and behaviour of the employee and less with rewarding or punishing specific aspects of the work performance. Under these circumstances the system of social control within the organisation changes (Townley, 1994). More emphasis is placed on rewarding teamwork and commitment and linking individuals' rewards to the performance of the organisation as a whole. The employer's agenda for training is widened from the traditional concerns of transmitting specific skills and coping with legal obligations, to creating identification with company objectives, implementing organisational change and ensuring adherence to quality standards (Felstead et al, 1997).

Although the evidence is still patchy and unsystematic, the main implications of these changes for the organisation of training are now becoming evident. Training departments are shrinking in size, relative to the parent organisation (American Society for Training and Development, 1996). In some instances the function has been out-sourced. This has been accompanied by a decline in the use of off-the-job training courses, both in the UK (Raper et al, 1997) and in the US (Bassi and Cheney, 1996). The responsibilities for training have been given to line managers and training has therefore become more focused on the needs of the line. Concomitant with this there has been an increase in mentoring, coaching and forms of structured on-the-job training (American Society for Training and Development, 1996; Raper et al, 1997). Trainers have been transformed into learning advisors and consultants or performance consultants, whose function is to advise line managers in the delivery of learning at work. Our own research and that in the US (American Society for Training and Development, 1996) has identified a range of new skills required for this role which include skills in: facilitating the process of learning; systems thinking and understanding; consultancy; and organisational development; and in addition a wider knowledge of business objectives and operational performance. Training is now increasingly seen as part of a process of lifelong learning and becomes part of a longer-term process of skill formation, which encompasses the moulding of attitudes and values as well as the transmission of specific skills.

Case Study 1

We use the following case study to demonstrate how these changes have reduced the role of formal one-off training courses and refocused attention on skill formation as a continuous process. It illustrates the mechanisms through which the structuring of the learning process has moved away from the training department and become focused on the

workplace. The establishment is part of a small, multinational company, engaged in the electronics manufacturing industries, combining some mass production with forms of batch production. In total it has over 4,000 employees in the UK and abroad. It operates in a very competitive market, facing strong competition from European companies. In order to survive it had to move from being production focused to being more responsive to its major customers and more innovative in the marketplace. This shift in company philosophy to a focus on the customer involved radical changes in the organisational culture and in the system of production.

Increases in productivity had been achieved through the redesign of the production process, for example, the eradication of stock; the use of Just In Time production; and the introduction of an integrated system of manufacture. Production was operated on the basis of cells with teams responsible for either the whole production process or a significant part. However, success depended on achieving higher levels of commitment on the part of the workforce to the company and its objectives and on a substantial part of the workforce acquiring problem solving, teamwork and management skills as identified above.

Transforming the company culture involved a basic change in the attitude of management toward the workforce. First it had to change its relationships with the unions. The company had three major unions and the first move from the Human Resources Director was to establish a relationship of trust between the company and the unions. This was achieved by opening the company's books to the unions and involving the union leadership and local officials in discussions about the problems facing the company and encouraging them to put forward proposals to overcome them. The unions responded in a positive manner: for example, when confronted with the need to improve productivity the unions suggested running the plant 52 weeks per year to improve productivity and took over responsibility for consulting members in order to minimise any inconvenience to their holiday arrangements. To ensure continued improvements in communication and the maintenance of a trusting relationship, site meetings were held every month with stewards and management representatives. This relationship of trust has underpinned many of the other human resources developments.

Employees' values and attitudes had to change to achieve the flexibility and willingness to operate effectively in teams, with the aim of enhancing company performance. In part this was achieved by the new relationship of trust between unions and employers. This was reinforced by a series of innovations designed to raise employees' awareness of the interdependence of the component parts of the organisation, and the importance of satisfying the customer to ensure the success of the organisation and therefore the security of their jobs. The first of these innovations was to dispense with the old system of teambuilding which involved sending staff on a two-day outdoor pursuits course at a cost of £6,000 per head, in the hope that teambuilding skills learned there would be transferred to the workplace. This was replaced by a two-day course designed in-house and aimed at demonstrating the problems of running a business. In particular it focused on the problems that each department faced with the aim of improving mutual understanding. In addition, the staff were put through a business game in which they had to compete with other teams in running a business. The aim was to demonstrate the interdependence of the various parts of the business and the importance of satisfying the customer. All staff, manual and non-manual, are currently being put through the course.

However, for the change in attitudes to be sustained through time, the company's commitment to open communication had to be reinforced. This was done through a system of monthly team briefings, the introduction of a company magazine and cross-functional management meetings to improve communication and mutual understanding of the component parts of the business. To involve staff more directly in the decision-making process, they all attended a course on continuous improvement which has been followed through with regular meetings where decisions on improvements are made in open forum.

The other component was to realign the system of rewards and punishments in accordance with the new emphasis on commitment to the organisation

through enhanced performance. Appraisals were introduced for all staff, use was made of relatively simple forms in order to minimise bureaucracy. The function of the appraisal was to identify barriers to improved performance – they were not linked to pay. This technique encouraged more effective upward communications from staff to supervisors. A substantial part of the training process is now devoted to sustaining the changes achieved in values and attitudes.

In the process of achieving this change training activities became focused more on the use of the workplace as a cost-effective means of transmitting the requisite skills for the 'new' organisation. Teamwork exercises were used to focus on team and individual performance and multiskilling was introduced in the form of training across a number of tasks to build in greater flexibility within each team.

Management education was changed. The old off-the-job courses delivered by external providers, which were not seen as linked to the company's needs, were replaced with a system of specialist one-off training sessions on specialist topics directly related to the manager's job, supplemented by enrolment on the Open University Effective Manager course, the fees for which are reimbursed on successful completion. For the technical staff, two programmes were run over 18 months. These use a combination of external experts and in-house courses for subjects such as contract law. These are assessed through a written examination, project work and presentation. Staff are paid £500 on successful completion, following which they are expected to demonstrate improved performance and the requisite behaviours before they are considered for promotion. Operatives receive their training on-the-job with most teams having a designated 'trainer' – a person who has successfully performed all the jobs in the team – who is responsible for the training of team members.

Responsibility for routine training was taken from the training department and given to the line managers. When new training needs are identified the training department is consulted for advice and help in constructing the course or programme, but the line manager is responsible for delivering the course. Training is now a component part of the business agenda and on the business reviews of line managers.

The effect of these changes has been dramatic. Training is more highly focused on improving company performance and the business objectives, productivity levels have improved and learning is now the responsibility of each manager (although not all managers were equally enthusiastic to acquire these new responsibilities). Training is no longer the exclusive province of the training department. The combined effect of these changes has been that the company has improved its market share from 13% to 26% in six years and reduced working hours from 39 to 37 per week.

There is no evidence from this particular case study that the level of skill formation within the organisation has increased. This may well have been the case, but the important point is that the system of skill formation is now tightly geared to the requirements of the business organisation. No doubt individuals in the past obtained some personal development from the outside courses but this was not closely linked to the requirements of the business. By replacing this and other forms of external courses with training at the workplace, which is tied more closely to improving performance, the company made continuous training an integral part of its activities rather than a series of one-off (frequently externally run) events which had only a tangential relationship to the person's job.

There is a danger with the use of case studies that we can over-generalise – this example is only used to illustrate a trend. Many organisations have not changed significantly, others contain elements of the old and the new. Where new forms have been introduced, certain elements of the old still persist: smaller centralised training units can coexist with learning consultants. In addition, much training and skill formation remains driven by traditional forces such as legal requirements, organisational procedures, and new technology (Felstead and Green, 1994). This case study simply highlights the direction of the trend.

If, as we have argued, training has become just one component of the skill formation process as learning at work has gained in prominence and employers

have become more concerned with shaping values and attitudes as well as job technical skills, what does this mean for the process of learning at work? Recent studies in the US (Darrah, 1996) and in Japan (Koike and Inoki, 1990) have started to explore this issue by focusing on the processes whereby individuals acquire skills in the course of their everyday work activities. Koike argues, on the basis of the Japanese experience, that high levels of skill formation can only be achieved through the use of work-based learning, especially through learning on-the-job. Eraut (1997) distinguishes between individual learning, the learning of a group and the learning organisation. We are concerned with the individual and group levels. At the level of group he defines learning capability as

> *... likely to comprise both overt shared understandings and procedures and tacit knowledge of working together creatively to define, solve and implement solutions to non-routine problems and issues. (p 10)*

In building on these studies we are asking the questions, how do individuals experience the process of learning, and how do the groups of which they are a part, as well as the organisation as a whole, shape it? These were questions addressed by the second of the case studies.

Case Study 2

The establishment was part of a large, Western, multinational company located in South East Asia. Semi-structured interviews were conducted with a representative sample of 195 of the 3,000 employees. The company had experienced re-engineering, involving a reduction in the headcount; a delayering of management; and the introduction of a new culture, where the focus was on enhancing efficiency through the adoption of a new way of working, geared to providing a better service to the customer. As the management sought to move the company in the direction of a 'learning organisation', responsibility for training had been devolved down the line, training was coordinated through the human resources and development function but the training department had been reduced dramatically in size as the trainers had been transformed into learning consultants. The company was widely recognised as being at the leading edge of developments in training within the region.

The interviews sought to explore all facets of learning at work, and what became evident was the problematic character of the process of learning at work. In order for learning to be effective, knowledge and information have to be shared, individuals have to be provided with the opportunity to apply the knowledge and practice new skills, support has to be provided in the form of effective feedback and, over the long term, the learning acquired has to be rewarded.

Within organisations learning takes place in the context of a variety of relationships with colleagues, superiors and subordinates and central to these relationships is the issue of trust. In the first case study, at the organisational level, building trust was seen as essential in gaining the commitment of the workforce to focus the process of skill formation on the goals of the enterprise. However, at the individual level, this is a problematic process. Although the second case study company had devoted considerable resources to communicating with employees, this was no guarantee of affecting change in individuals' behaviour and attitudes. Much of the communication was mediated by the supervisor or manager and if the relationship with the supervisor or manager is one where the manager is "fussy", "doesn't trust us", "doesn't care", "shows no interest in staff", there is little impetus for the staff to identify with the organisation or to learn. Even in organisations which have delayered, hierarchy is still a central feature of everyday experience and has a profound effect on the learning process. It was not uncommon that learning was hindered by bosses who did not trust their subordinates and were reluctant to share information and knowledge. As one manager remarked, "knowledge is power, people are selfish and this is more so at the middle and lower levels". However, this was not always the case; other managers were careful to bring on their staff – "staff must understand your style. They share a lot more, including mistakes. You have to approach them, have a chit-chat". As with many organisations undergoing change, there were certain groups of managers in both our case study organisations who were reluctant to share knowledge.

Similarly, if the relationship with colleagues is competitive, trust cannot develop and there is little incentive to share experiences and knowledge, to support colleagues in their attempts to develop their skills, or to build the learning capability of the group to which Eraut refers (1997). In some instances this was a case of "people are willing to share provided they are the right person", or,

"If you know the person there is no difficulty in getting information. You have to do a lot of networking. Bosses might not understand this."

In other instances, where teams were functioning effectively, learning at the group level was taking place and the sharing of knowledge and information among colleagues was not a problem, "We are in a team, we sink or swim together, so there are no problems in sharing knowledge". Significantly, in project work where the teams were created for a specific purpose, the sharing of knowledge was least problematic.

When it came to opportunities to apply new knowledge and practice skills, two main issues emerged from the data concerning the factors which influenced this dimension of skill formation. The first was the structural issue of whether senior management grouped tasks in such a way as to provide for individual progression in their learning in the manner outlined by Koike and Inoki (1990), or whether individuals were allocated to different tasks in what appeared to them to be a fairly random process which did not enable them to build up skills progressively during the course of their employment with the company. In the case of management, there was considerable thought put into the development of senior staff to ensure that they acquired the appropriate experience, thus young graduates would report that their job movements within the company had 'broadened their experience', as they moved from technical jobs to supervising sub-contractors to jobs involving more managerial skills. However, for those lower down, in clerical jobs, this had not been the case. It appeared to the employees that they were moved around in a fairly random manner, in such a way that the skills acquired in one job were lost when they moved to another where they had to acquire another unrelated set of competencies, thus militating against cumulative learning at the individual level. The more widespread use of teamwork may reduce this as the individual's job movement is likely to be to different jobs within the same workgroup.

The second issue when it came to practising new skills concerned the individual's relationship with their immediate superior. In some instances bosses were reluctant to delegate authority and thereby provide the employee with the opportunity to acquire and practise new skills.

"If the boss has delegated it to you, you should be fully responsible. Some bosses never trust the individual.... You feel your boss has no confidence in you."

In another instance an employee commented that his boss "tackles all the difficult stuff himself", the employee was never given the opportunity to extend his knowledge and skills. This is clearly related to the issue of trust but also represents a serious barrier to the process of skill formation.

An individual may have knowledge and opportunity to practise but for learning to continue support is required, either from colleagues or supervisors, depending on the context. Again two major issues emerged from the interviews. The first concerned belief among certain sectors that learning itself was unproblematic, a 'natural' process which occurs of its own accord that did not require any special support or consideration. This led to a belief in some quarters that new entrants, especially graduates, should not be 'spoonfed' and that they learn by being 'thrown in at the deep end'. Where this was the case the learner was unlikely to receive further support.

The second issue concerned the lack of knowledge among managers and others about how to support the learning process. The significance of appropriate feedback, especially in the workplace, has been well established by Koike and Inoki (1990). If staff are not provided with feedback on how well they are performing the process of learning becomes haphazard. Some employees had weekly meetings to obtain feedback on their performance. However, although many staff were aware of the importance of receiving feedback so that learning could proceed in anything other than an ad hoc manner, the significance of this feedback was not always

recognised by those involved in the learning process. As one employee put it, what you require is "A listening ear, open, not judgmental, able to empathise and give guidance, provide guidelines". What she did not want from her supervisor was

"... someone who argues with you rather than listens to the problem, who shoots you down saying 'You should have done this'. When that happens, you feel depressed and feel the exercise was a waste of time."

Finally, learning can be a rewarding activity in its own right, in that the individual feels a sense of achievement and positive learning experiences enhance self-confidence. However, from the organisation's point of view, if the process of skill formation is to be geared to business objectives, learning that is related to the achievement of these objects requires rewarding and reinforcing. The interesting finding from the interviews was that in the short term the main reward the individuals mentioned was just a 'thank you' or acknowledgement from the superior. Of course, in the longer term this was seen as insufficient in that most of the staff would prefer a concrete reward in the form of progression or promotion.

From the employees' perspective, within this company formal training was an infrequent activity but learning was an everyday occurrence. The company was attempting to move in the direction of a 'learning organisation' but the evidence suggested that this was a problematic process. Employees faced many barriers in their efforts to learn, not because the company deliberately erected them, indeed the company were unaware of them, but because the process of learning is contentious, with the parties involved having different agendas and in many instances not being aware of how to facilitate the process. At each stage in the process – in the sharing of knowledge; in the provision of opportunities for practice; in the support of the learning process; and in the rewarding of it – the process can be easily fractured.

Conclusions

The case for conceptualising skill formation as a continuous process through time in which learning at work is central rather than a series of discontinuous, one-off educational or training activities, derives not only from an academic need to broaden the research agenda but from concrete changes taking place in the workplace. As we have seen, organisational changes are making the process of learning at work more central to the achievement of business objectives. Active involvement in the process is extending beyond trainers to include managers, supervisors and employees, in ways never envisaged before. For trainers, especially those whose role has been transformed into 'learning consultants', and who now find themselves with the new tasks of facilitating the learning process, advising managers on how to identify learning needs and to support the process of learning in the workplace, new skills in consultancy and the management of the learning process are urgently required.

Yet despite these changes, many of those directly involved in the process of learning at work, both managers and individuals, still tend to see learning as relatively unproblematic, a natural occurrence which requires little support. One major implication of this is that we need to develop more adequate theories of learning in the workplace. Conventional theories of 'learning by osmosis' or 'learning by doing' deflect attention from the complexities of the processes we observe. Learning theories derived from experimental observations and studies of the cognitive process abstracted from the realities of the organisational context are of little relevance to the practitioner, or for that matter, the academic struggling to understand the process of learning as embedded in organisational structures.

Eraut has made a useful start on reconceptualising the agenda by drawing our attention to the range of learning which takes place at work and the fact that the process of learning is more specific than merely absorbing information.

> *Learning should refer only to significant changes in capability or understanding and exclude the acquisition of further information when it does not contribute to such changes. (Eraut, 1997)*

Such a definition focuses attention more clearly on the central issues at both the individual and group level. However, it also raises the question of whether the changes in attitudes and values necessary for ensuring the commitment of the individual to both the group and the wider organisation, should also be a component part of this process of learning? Without that commitment, much of the learning, especially at the group level and above, cannot take place. Other important contributions have been made by Koike in his studies of learning at work (1997), but in focusing on the conditions in Japanese organisations which facilitate the process of skill acquisition, he tends to ignore the conflicts and struggles which are also involved in the process. Nevertheless, these are important contributions which serve to highlight the urgent need for academics to provide a more adequate conceptualisation to guide both theory and practice, and in so doing broaden the research agenda away from its current preoccupation with education and training as the main components of the skill formation process. Practitioners in the field are in urgent need of the help such research could provide.

Author's acknowledgements

The author wishes to acknowledge the helpful comments of Frank Coffield on an earlier draft and Linda Jones who conducted the fieldwork on which the second case study was based.

Notes

[1] See, for example, Osterman (1995). The author is aware of the significance of informal on-the-job training, but given the difficulties of measuring informal learning is obliged to concentrate his data collection and subsequent analysis on formal off-the-job training.

[2] These observations are derived from an ongoing research project on the impact of organisational change on the organisation of training and learning at work. To date the project has involved detailed interviews with trainers and other employees in 48 organisations within the UK. The organisations covered a range of industries in the manufacturing, service and public sectors. The organisations ranged

in size from large multinationals to relatively small, local organisations with a total of 64 employees. The interviews were usually with senior trainers in the larger organisations and those responsible for training in smaller organisations; they also included some interviews with other shopfloor or office employees.

[3] These 'competences' are now to be found in a more formalised form in the publications of the DfEE and the Confederation of British Industry (CBI) (see Parsons and Marshall, 1996; CBI, 1995).

References

American Society for Training and Development (1996) *Trends that affect corporate learning and performance*, Alexandria: ASTD.

Bassi, L.J. and Cheney, S. (1996) *Restructuring: Results from the 1996 Forum*, Alexandria: ASTD.

Bertrand, O. and Noyelle, T. (1989) *Human resources and corporate strategy: Technological change in banks and insurance companies*, Paris: OECD.

CBI (Confederation of British Industry) (1995) *Realising a vision: A skills passport*, London: CBI.

Darrah, C.N. (1996) *Learning and work: An exploration in industrial ethnography*, London: Garland Publishing.

Eraut, M. (1997) 'Perspectives on defining "The Learning Society"', Paper prepared for the ESRC Learning Society Programme, Brighton: Institute of Education, University of Sussex.

Felstead, A. and Green, F. (1994) 'Training during the recession,' *Work, Employment and Society*, vol 8, no 2, pp 199-219.

Felstead, A., Green, F. and Mayhew, K. (1997) *Getting the measure of training: A report on training statistics in Britain*, Leeds: Centre for Industrial Policy and Performance, University of Leeds.

Kelly, M.R. (1989) 'Alternative forms of work organization under programmable automation', in S. Wood (ed) *The transformation of work*, London: Unwin Hyman.

Koike, K. (1997) *Human resource management*, Tokyo: Japan Institute of Labour.

Koike, K. and Inoki, T. (eds) (1990) *Skill formation in Japan and Southeast Asia*, Tokyo: Tokyo University Press.

Lawler, E.E. (1994) 'From job-based to competence-based organisations', *Journal of Organizational Behaviour*, vol 15, no 2, pp 3-15.

Osterman, P. (1995) 'Skill, training and work organisation in American establishments', *Industrial Relations*, vol 34, no 2, pp 125-46.

O'Reilly, J. (1992) 'Where do you draw the line? Functional flexibility, training and skill in Britain and France', *Work, Employment and Society*, vol 6, no 3, pp 369-96.

Parsons, D. and Marshall, V. (1996) *Skills, qualifications and utilisation: A research review*, DfEE Research Series No 67, Sheffield: DfEE.

Raper, P., Ashton, D., Felstead, A. and Storey, J. (1997) 'Toward the learning organisation? Explaining current trends in training practice in the UK', *International Journal of Training and Development*, vol 1, no 1, pp 9-21.

Townley, B. (1994) *Reframing human resource management: Power, ethics and the subject at work*, London: Sage.

Thompson, P., Wallace, T., Flecker, G. and Ahlstraand, R. (1995) 'It ain't what you do, it's the way that you do it: production organisation and skill utilisation in commercial vehicles', *Work, Employment and Society*, vol 9, no 4, pp 719-42.

Learning Resources
Centre